SPAIN ON A PLATE

María José Sevilla's passion for Spanish food and wine is rooted in her Basque country origins. From there she has travelled throughout Spain, learning about regional food and ingredients from local people and collecting many of the delicious recipes to be found in this book.

An acknowledged expert on Spanish food and wine, María José presented the BBC television series *Spain on a Plate* which won a Glenfiddich award in 1992. She is also the author of *Life and Food in the Basque Country* (Weidenfeld & Nicolson). Since 1974, María José has been involved with promoting Spanish food and wine through the Commercial Office of the Spanish Embassy in London.

SPAIN ON A PLATE

The best of
Spanish regional food

María José Sevilla

BBC Books

Without the support and backing of: Juan Calabozo, Commercial Counsellor at the Spanish Embassy in London; Patrick Gooch, Director of Foods from Spain; Dick Foster, producer of *Spain on a Plate*; Janine Gilson, colleague and translator; Vicky Hayward, friend and literary consultant; Suzanne Webber and Nicky Copeland from BBC Books; and Wendy Hobson who has not only tested all the recipes but edited the complete work, without those people, this book would not have been possible. Nor without my son, Daniel, and his constant cups of tea and coffee, nor my mother, Angeles and her love for food.

Published by BBC Books,
a division of BBC Enterprises Limited
Woodlands, 80 Wood Lane, London W12 0TT

ISBN 0 563 37038 6

Editor and home economist: Wendy Hobson
Map by Technical Art Services
Illustrations by Kate Simunek

Set by Phoenix Photosetting, Chatham, Kent
Printed and bound in Great Britain by Clays Ltd, St Ives plc

CONTENTS

NOTES ON THE RECIPES

Follow one set of measurements only, do not mix metric and imperial.

All eggs used are size 2.

Wash fresh produce before preparation.

Spoon measurements are level unless otherwise specified.

Adjust seasoning and strongly flavoured ingredients, such as onions and garlic, to suit your own taste.

If you substitute dried for fresh herbs, use only half the amount specified.

Recipes suitable for vegetarians are indicated by a Ⓥ symbol. Please note that these recipes may include cheese and other dairy products.

Most of the ingredients used in the recipes are available in supermarkets or delicatessens. Suitable alternatives and some of the cooking techniques are listed in the recipes or in the glossary. If you do have any problems obtaining specific ingredients, contact: Foods from Spain, Spanish Embassy Commercial Office, 66 Chiltern Street, London, W1M 1PR.

INTRODUCTION

The sound of the pestle rings out only in the memory of the country women of Catalonia and Andalusia, who have been pounding tomato and cucumber in marble or stone mortars since time immemorial. The summer *gazpachos* and almond *picada* sauces that are made for Catalan seafood stews from finely ground ingredients are still part of the Spanish cooking scenario, but the pestle has long since been replaced by the electric blender. Despite this, and a hundred other similar changes, Spanish culinary traditions – scarcely known in the rest of Europe – have managed to survive intact. I hope to introduce them to you.

My father's surname, apparently Jewish Sephardi in origin, was Sevilla. He was an army man and a traveller, and every four or five years my mother would pack up our trunks and summon a removal van. During my childhood and adolescence, I remember living in Madrid, the Canary Islands, Andalusia, Valencia, Extremadura, then back again in 'my town', as I think of Madrid. My mother inherited her style of cooking from her mother, a Navarrese by birth and an excellent cook. Her expertise was further enriched by the influence of the traditions and ingredients she would discover on her daily visits to the markets and through her conversations with people about food.

Over the last ten years, I have continued to travel around Spain, at first in search of vines and knowledge about how to make good wine, more recently in pursuit of cooking styles, *cocinas* as we call them, and anything else I can learn about the best of Spanish food and drink.

The fact that Spain has spent so much of her history overrun by outsiders might at first appear a disadvantage from a culinary point of view. The result, however, has been that Spanish cooking has absorbed a range of quite wonderful and different cooking styles and made them her own. Some are simple, others more complex, but in all the quality and freshness of the ingredients are paramount.

I talk about *cocinas* in the plural because Spain can be divided into a number of gastronomic regions. These imaginary divisions have very little to do with those established by the politicians. Rather they have come about because of the development of different local traditions, each enriched in various ways by the Greek, Carthaginian, Roman and Moorish cultures, as well as by the abundant new produce brought from the Americas. This book is not an attempt to give a deep study of these gastronomic regions, but instead tries to depict some of the most striking features of the regions, and to offer you those recipes that I consider to be the most characteristic.

You will find that my sketches bear little or no resemblance to the images of the cooking styles of my country that have been established by the tourist industry. Perhaps because the industry has been too timid, visitors have not always been able to look properly at what the country really has to offer in terms of food and wine. I can assure you that our native taste has very little to do with what is often served up under the name of *gazpacho, paella* or *sangría*. In reality it is all about roast peppers, seafood, wonderful rice dishes, Serrano ham, Asturian bean stews, peaches from Aragón, fresh Mediterranean herbs from Mallorca, and the wines of Rioja, Navarra, Cambados or Penedés.

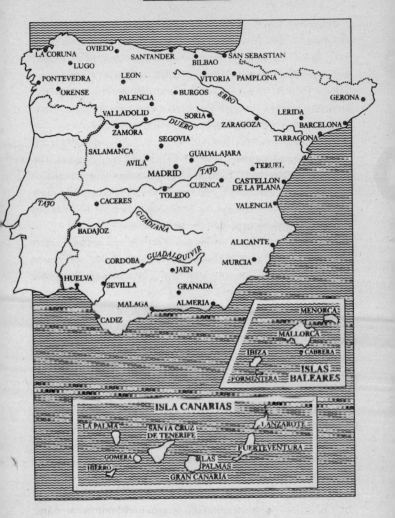

These are just hints of what is to come. We will look at –
and taste – fishermen's stews cooked in earthenware pots,
fresh fish fried to perfection in olive oil, chick peas cooked
with spinach, *empanada* pies made for festive occasions,
onions roasted over hot coals, and dishes created in the
workshops of the professional cooks who have done so much
to update recipes with traditional village flavours.

Previously these recipes had been passed down orally from
farmhouse and hamlet, from the plains of Andalusia in the
south to the northern Cantabrian mountains, always encap-
sulating the flavours of the countryside. Today, the new
versions may sometimes take on European or Mediterranean
city airs, but they preserve the original spirit.

The various cooking styles smell of fish and seafood fresh
from the sea, of seasoned roast meat, and of the rich wines
that are used in country chicken and partridge hotpots.
There are Mediterranean styles: olive green in colour, and
tasting of olive oil and almonds, rice and saffron. There are
other styles that reflect the interior with its mountains and
shepherds, cheeses and honey, and pinto beans cooked in
deep, painted metal and enamel *pucheros*. Different again is
the cookery of the villages that are snowbound in the winter,
with flavours of rich stock and pork fat; of villages that
slumber on in the silence of Castile, the so-called lands of
bread and wine; and those that bustle in vivacious Andalusia.

These are the *cocinas* of Spain, developed from family, bar
and restaurant cooking, which have survived both the
changes that have swept through the Peninsula's kitchens and
the influence of some untalented innovators. Now, with the
help of some true professionals, guardians of our culture and
lovers of the quality food and wine of my country, the real
spirit of Spanish cookery is reborn.

ANDALUSIA

When I think of Andalusia, I do not think only of the sea. Instead I imagine wheat fields, sunflower plantations, vineyards and olive groves, rolling hills and mountains, exuberant patios bursting with green plants, sweet fresh water, tranquillity and light – a special light that is an inspiration to me. I also imagine balconies laden with multi-coloured geraniums, and the fragrance of orange blossom accompanying me along the roads that lead away into distant gorges, mountain ranges and meadows of incomparable beauty. Add to this scene parcels of fried fish from Cádiz, cold almond soup from Córdoba or Málaga, and olive oil, garlic and tomatoes – the three staple ingredients of Andalusian cooking – and the picture begins to emerge.

Family and religion, food and wine; these are the four pillars that still support the fabric of Andalusia's social life. The region has a rich culinary tradition that encompasses the widely disparate lore of the peoples of Al-Andalus, the name given by the Moors to Seville, Cordoba, Granada, Almería, Cádiz, Málaga, Jaén and Huelva.

This Andalusian tradition is often narrowly summed up as 'fried food' and denigrated both by the rest of Spain and by those beyond the Pyrenees as being the Peninsula's poorest and most primitive. To those who make such comments, I recommend taking another look, for they are likely to find what I did a long time ago: an exciting and delicious taste experience.

It would be impossible to begin to talk about Andalusia's cooking styles without first looking briefly at this land where one of Europe's earliest civilized peoples lived in the fertile basin of the romantic Guadalquivir river. We must consider too, the history of the peoples that invaded Andalusia, fell in love with and, in many cases, enriched it.

The heritage of the Phoenicians, Carthaginians, Romans and, to a certain extent, the Jews is evident in Andalusian food. But overshadowing all these, is the heritage of the Moors. Their legacy of *majados* or pounding food, fried food and bitter-sweet flavours is an essential part of Andalusian gastronomy.

The Ancient Phoenicians were responsible for planting the vine in Andalusia, and today we have one of the greatest white wines of the world: sherry. They also left us saffron, the spice we adore. The Carthaginians introduced the chick pea which is so popular throughout Spain. The Romans installed the first irrigation systems, bringing life to an arid country, planted fruits and vegetables, and created our fishing industry. It was they, too, who first cultivated the olive tree, which until then had grown gloriously wild in Jaén and Córdoba.

Amongst the multitude of foods introduced by the Moors are figs and pomegranates, bitter oranges and melons, spinach and aubergines, rice and almonds. During their 700-year stay in the Peninsula they developed an excellent culinary repertoire, making use of a wealth of spices and preparations unknown to the rest of Europe, which slumbered on amid the 'delights' of medieval cooking. The Moors gave to the food of Andalusia its most characteristic flavours and to its people their beautiful eyes and olive skins.

In Andalusia the cooking is born of little money, yet it is as seductive and joyfully resourceful as are the people of the towns and villages. Do not expect great Basque or Catalan-style elaborations in Andalusian cooking; it is simple and comes from the heart.

The clear exception to this, however, is found in Jerez, where cooking has been strongly influenced by the French, and has even absorbed a few English methods and dishes which arrived in association with the sherry trade. These were maintained by the local aristocracy in what undoubtedly remains, even today, a feudal society.

One of the most outstanding aspects of traditional Anda-lusian cooking is the soups, especially the cold soups which refresh the palate in the hot summers. The Andaulusians love them.

Despite what some people maintain, they are not all *gaz-pachos*. In Andalusian, the term *gazpacho* should only be used for a cold dish of liquid consistency, often drunk from a glass, containing tomato and bread, along with garlic, olive oil, vinegar and water; peppers and cucumber are optional. Until just a few years ago, *gazpachos* were always made by pounding the ingredients one by one to a smooth paste, which was then usually diluted with water. This work was done by the *casera*, the woman who cooks for the teams of labourers working in the fields. Today, even in the most remote places, electric blenders have to a large extent replaced this traditional method. Nonetheless, people still anxiously await the arrival of the year's first tomatoes in June, the herald of the *gazpacho* season. The delicious white garlic speciality from Málaga, *ajo blanco, porra* from Antequera, and *salmorejo* from Córdoba are not *gazpachos*, as they all differ in their ingredients, consistency, or both.

Not all Andalusian soups are cold: many a time in a friend's house or in a simple restaurant I have enjoyed hot soup and vegetable or fish stews of the sort in which the fishermen of

Sanlúcar excel. In Andalusia, *cocidos*, when everything is cooked in one pot, can be made with six different kinds of vegetable, apart from the traditional meat and pork. The vegetables chosen depend on the time of year, and may include chard, cabbage, broad beans, peas, green beans, and *boronia* or *alboronia*, a Moorish combination of aubergine, pumpkin, capsicum and tomato, which can also be made into a sauce. The authentic Moorish version is spiced with coriander, cumin and saffron.

Five of the eight provinces of Andalusia – Huelva, Cádiz, Málaga, Granada and Almería – are poised on the edge of the Atlantic or the Mediterranean, and each has more than a romantic association with fishing. Fish baked in salt is not the exclusive preserve of southern Spain, but in Seville and Cádiz it is irresistible. Be it sea bass, grouper, large red mullet or gilt-head bream, the fish retains all its flavour when cooked by this simple method and only absorbs the salt it needs.

There is no doubt that the Andalusians know how to fry fish, particularly in Cádiz and Málaga. Simple fish caught only a short way offshore are preferred: hake steaks, *filetes de merluza*; small hake, *pescadilla*; *pixotas* which are even tastier hake; *acedías* or wedge sole; anchovies which are tied together by the tail in fans of six at a time; and *cazón*, a very tasty dogfish which is usually marinated overnight in vinegar, garlic, cumin and coriander before frying. Squid rings are also very popular, just dipped in flour, salted and dashed in very hot olive oil.

The great secret of frying fish as they do in the Andalusian *freidurías*, or street frying shops, is to use a large pan and plenty of very hot olive oil. Several kinds of fish are cooked at once, just for a short time. Those who know about frying insist that a properly cooked fish can virtually be popped from the pan into your pocket without making it greasy.

Shellfish are also excellent along these shores and the *langostinos* from Sanlúcar, the *camarones* or prawns, and the *quisquillas* or shrimps are in themselves worth a trip to Cádiz.

The great wealth of fish that enlivens the cooking of this region is comparable only to the variety of pork products that are made in Al-Andalus, particularly in Granada and the sierras of Huelva. The small town of Jabugo is perched at more than 800 metres above the sea in the fabulous Sierra de Aracena in the province of Huelva. Its name is well known to any self-respecting Spaniard who can pay the prices demanded for the cured ham, *chorizo* sausage and black pudding made here and in the immediate vicinity.

Fresh and cured pork products from here or elsewhere are a very important part of a culinary tradition which includes few other meat dishes. Game is also popular, as it is abundant in the mountains and sea marshes of southern Spain. A good example is wild duck, which is cooked with olives in Seville, or the many variations of small game dishes cooked in vegetable sauces which are available during the shooting season in the local *ventas* or inns.

Apart from fruit, a crème caramel and one or two puddings, little else is commendable at dessert time in the region. But, as if to compensate, the Moorish and Jewish traditions bequeathed to Al-Andalus an unparalleled legacy of confectionery that survives in the pastry shops and, most especially, in the convents of closed religious orders. The recipes are transmitted by word of mouth from nun to nun and are a closely guarded secret – which makes them all the more interesting to me.

My personal favourites are the almond pastries made by the barefoot Carmelites in Jerez, but I have also tasted crumbly shortcake, butter cakes, wine rings, curls, gypsy's arm, vanilla laces, puff pastries, coconut delicacies, jams, quince paste, almond and cinnamon confections, sesame puffs, marzipan flowers – the list runs on and on.

Possibly the most famous of all these sweets are the *yemas*, delicacies made from egg yolks by the nuns of the convent of San Leandro in Seville. There is also a wonderful pastry shop, the Pastelería La Esperanza, in the Calle de las Bodegas in Jerez, which specializes in egg yolk sweets. Up until ten short years ago, the sherry houses clarified their wines with egg whites and the yolks that were left used to be sold at very modest prices. The introduction of new vinification technology has meant that this efficient but rudimentary method of clarification has ceased to exist. As a result, the price of the confectionery has doubled and I fear that eventually the nuns will be the only guardians of this ancient and wonderful tradition.

MADRID
AND THE
MESETAS

Little Chinese lanterns and paper chains criss-cross the ebullient street. The façades of the buildings, their balconies bright with flowers and draped with Manilla shawls, have sprung to life. La Florida is celebrating a festival, praying and singing in honour of Saint Anthony, its patron saint and protector of lovers. Along the broad esplanade, children and adults are buying sweets from street-sellers: the memorable sticks of rock known as *bastones de caramelo*, liquorice, little doughnuts called *rosquillas*, toffee apples and sugared almonds. This is one of Madrid's most famous *verbenas*, or street festivals, which I remember so well from my childhood in the city.

Apparently the *verbenas* originated in the eleventh century when Madrid used to make merry, celebrating what were originally religious festivals. I have been lucky enough to experience the three most famous: La Paloma, San Isidro and San Antonio de la Florida. Still vivid in my mind is the traditional *barquillero*. This colourful figure, dressed in a typical nineteenth-century Madrileño outfit, used to follow the *verbenas* selling, for one peseta, delicious *barquillos*, fine rolled wafer leaves made with flour, sugar, lard, egg yolks, water and lemon or cinnamon.

Capital of the kingdom since Philip II, a Habsburg, decided to settle his court in the centre of the Peninsula, Madrid divides the central *meseta* or plateau of Spain into its two Castiles. North of Madrid is the Castile that is epitomized by roast dishes, and which produces the high quality wines of the Duero and the wonderful black puddings of Burgos. To the south lies the Castile of La Mancha cheeses, Toledo marzipan and the lively wines of Valdepeñas.

Even though the bustling European Madrid of today has lost some of the attractions of twenty years ago, it is still a place I find exciting to visit. The best place to explore is the city's oldest quarter, called de los Austrias because it dates from the time of the Austrian monarchs. Here you can taste the best of Spain's regional cooking, including, of course, that of the *meseta* to which Madrid's specialities belong.

On an ordinary weekday you would think that the Calle de Cuchilleros, twisting its way down from the lovely San Miguel Market, is just like any of the multitude of other streets in Old Madrid. After dark on Friday and Saturday, though, it is one of the city's busiest streets. Take away a couple of flamenco *tablados* or stages and their tourist spirit, and you find a number of *mesones*, old Castilian inns, frequented by the young and impecunious who can spend hours over a plate of mushrooms and a glass of the house wine, or meandering between several different places in search of music and friendly faces. In my day, this was what we called *ir de mesones*, to go on a crawl around the *mesones*, eating, drinking and above all socializing. This is, roughly speaking, a Castilian version of a *tapas* crawl – hopping round the city's delightful bars, drinking, eating delicious snacks and absorbing the atmosphere as you go.

Madrid still sports a multitude of bars where the Andalusian *tapa*, adapted to city ways and tastes, reigns in delectable supremacy. Some bars can boast long-established, often life-long, customers. Such is the Bar Santander in the downtown area called Chueca. Every day the brothers who own it decorate the counter so beautifully that, cosmopolitan *tapas* crawler though I may be, I am unable to think of any other in Spain that could compare. At ten-thirty in the morning the first customers arrive for their coffee, beer or *aguardiente* and, always, something to eat. This may be one or two *pinchos*, pieces of bread topped with Manchego cheese or *chorizo* sausage from Extremadura, salt cod fritters or tuna and tomato pastries, the speciality of the house. There are dozens of this kind of establishment in the city, and they ideally suit the Madrileños' predilection for street life.

In other areas, where large modern buildings share their space with luxurious and beautiful edifices of Bourbon Madrid and with the latest architects' creations, the format is different – but the essence is the same. Come eleven o'clock, office workers dash in and out for their second breakfast: a quick jaunt for coffee and a bite to eat is almost compulsory, and many a blind eye is turned to allow it. This is a splendid custom that I have sorely misssed for twenty years now. The same bars will be full again between one and two in the afternoon, with one difference: the customers will drink beer instead of coffee, but they will nibble at food just the same.

Between half-past two and half-past six in the afternoon is a particularly quiet time during the summer months when the city is either on holiday, or those of its residents who have stayed behind are asleep or at work (in air-conditioned offices if they are lucky). Then Madrid gets itself into gear again. This is *cafetería* time, when the women who have been out window-shopping together and the couples who are on their daily walk about the city centre go in for tea, the *merienda*. They will have coffee and cake or pastries; pancakes covered with chocolate, caramel or strawberry sauce; or sandwiches filled with Russian salad, Cabrales blue cheese or one of some dozen other tasty versions.

The whole area around the Puerta Cerrada and Plaza Mayor is evocative of the early establishments where travellers would go to eat at modest prices. You will also find there *mesones* that specialize in one thing, for instance omelettes or mushrooms, and local restaurants, such as Botín, that are now famous.

Botín dates back to the sixteenth century. Its specialities are lamb and suckling pig roasted in a huge wood-fired baker's oven. Roasting very young and tender lamb is an art which has come down to us from the times of the Romans ar d early Christian kings. It is practised almost exclusively by the Castilians of the high *meseta*: Segovia, Peñaranda de Duero, Sepúlveda, Cuenca, beautiful Tordesillas, Peñafiel and Aranda – are all towns and cities whose names are deeply linked with this tradition.

Botín's menu also takes us on a tour of the food of Castile and Madrid, introducing us to dishes such as baked sea bream, a typical Christmas treat; Toledo partridges cooked in a *cazuela*; simple yet delicious soups of garlic and bread; and San Isidro salad made with lettuce, hard-boiled eggs and olives with *escabeche*, tuna fish cured and marinated in vinegar, oil and garlic.

A few of the typical inexpensive family establishments can still be found among the ultra-modern and more luxurious restaurants in the central areas of the city. Their role is to feed the innumerable students and travellers, as well as anyone else who misses their mother's home cooking. For very modest prices, you can eat down-to-earth three-course meals: excellent lentils to start; breaded cutlets as a main course; followed by fruit or flan plus bread and wine.

Lentils are as old as broad beans, and were loved by the Romans and the Ancient Spaniards, who liked to eat them with pork products such as black pudding and sausages. My mother used to add a little piece of ham and a carrot to give extra flavour and colour or, on days of abstinence, a few grains of rice. Vegetable dishes such as chard in winter and cauliflower all year round were also often served as a first course.

Few places do not serve the dish of Madrid, the *cocido madrileño* – pulses, vegetables and meat cooked in one pot to create a complete meal, including a substantial broth. The romantically inclined say that *cocido* was a Celtiberian dish, made by those first inhabitants of Hispania. Certainly it has come down to us today with Galician, Catalan, mountain and Andalusian names, and is made the length and breadth of my country. People disagree about its origins. Some maintain that it derives from the Sephardi Jewish dish called *adafina* or *dafina*. My own opinion is that, given its simplicity and common sense, it appeared spontaneously, created out of making the most of what was available at the time.

Porras for breakfast and *churros* and chocolate for tea are other great Madrileño customs and still favourites in my imaginary book of rich, fattening and utterly irresistible foods. I enjoy *porras* with my morning milky coffee, and I am quite capable of running around five or six bars to find some. Both *porras* and *churros* are made from the same batter, but *churros* are smaller, ridged on the outside and have a different texture. *Churros* are part of what I call the *fruta de sartén*, literally the fruits of the frying-pan. They are made with a light flour and water batter, fried and dusted with a little sugar. The *churro* is given its typical shape by the metal or wooden pipe through which the *churrero*, or churro-maker, forces the batter out into a vat of very hot olive oil.

Drinking chocolate is frequently enjoyed in city cafés with the *churros*. In my grandparents' day, it used to be served with *picatostes*, little sticks of bread soaked in milk and fried, toasted bread, or *bizcochos de Soletilla*, little cakes made of milk, egg and flour. Chocolate was brought to Spain from Mexico by the conquistadores at the beginning of the sixteenth century. The drink the Aztecs used to prepare was bitter and unpleasant, but once in the hands of the Spanish nuns at a covent in Guajaca, the same basic ingredient, cocoa, was transformed into a state secret that was sold to the French by Philip V in 1728. The drink *par excellence* of the Spanish Golden Age in the sixteenth and seventeenth centuries, it was served as part of something called *agasajo*, a snack which usually included crystallized fruits, sponge cakes and marzipans.

The tea biscuits, cakes and tiny fruit pastries purveyed in the *pâtisseries* of Madrid stand very fair comparison with the best made in any other city of Europe, but there are one or two outstanding local specialities: *bartolillos* and *canutillos*. Both are fried pastries filled with confectioner's custard. The pastry for the triangular *bartolillos* is made with olive oil, a little lard, eggs, flour and sugar, while the *canutillos* are made with milk, olive oil, a few drops of vinegar, flour and salt, giving them a very different texture.

Fresh strawberries are another treat of the city, both the large *fresones* and the minute *fresas*, which are cultivated but also grow wild at Aranjuez, once the summer residence of the Spanish monarchs. Sugared almonds from Alcalá de Henares, an important university city, are also typical of Madrid. Both complement the excellent Manchego cheese, so ubiquitous in the gastronomy of Castile.

CATALONIA

My culinary wandering through one of the finest regions of the Peninsula began in the dining-room of a delightful *masía* or farmstead on a vineyard in the Alto Penedés. Only years later did I discover Barcelona, one of Spain's most exciting cities, specifically the Barceloneta, a working-class port area where I was fortunate enough to spend several enchanting months.

Bounded by the Pyrenees to the north, the fertile delta of the Ebro to the south, the kingdom of Aragón to the west and the Mediterranean to the east, Catalonia – possibly the wealthiest and most European of the regions of Spain – lies in the north-east of the Peninsula. The mountains and the sea were destined to become the major influences on the gastronomy of Catalonia's four provinces: Gerona, Barcelona, Lérida and Tarragona. The enormous variety of their landscapes gives us ample scope to talk about such things as palm hearts and fig trees in Tarragona, prickly pears and bilberries in Gerona, rice and wild ducks along the Ebro, and partridges and woodland mushrooms from the Pyrenees.

When I returned to Barcelona at the end of the seventies after a long absence, I found a relatively new and unfamiliar style of cooking, far removed from the cookery of the ordinary people that was described to me with such enthusiasm in the bars and restaurants of the Barceloneta. It was also a far cry from the old Catalan festive cooking which was mentioned in treatises dating back before the sixteenth century. For by the seventies the splendid eating houses had disappeared and women's way of life and role in society had undergone major changes. Most homes and restaurants were producing food with international overtones, or at least greatly influenced by other cultures, but which was also less complex than the indigenous, rural cooking that had begun to disappear in the fifties when Spain was still in the throes of its own post-war period.

Barcelona is a beautiful Mediterranean city with a flavour of merchant shipping and adventure. It thrives on political debate, but it is also profoundly bourgeois and industrial. Its people have eclectic taste: they love pasta, rice and salt cod, and they have lunch and dinner and go to bed earlier than anybody else in Spain. In the last ten years, though, their appetite has woken up. Now, the people are frequenting restaurants that are amongst Spain's best. These establishments have gained European recognition for their artistic and innovative ability, although these qualities are nothing new in this lively city. The Catalans enjoy the traditional cooking of restaurants in the Barrio Gótico, the Gothic quarter, as much as the ultra-modern creations to be found in the Via Augusta.

When it comes to eating, Catalans in general, and the people of Barcelona in particular, are very demanding – proof of which is evident in the quality of the *tapas* and other dishes served in bars and restaurants all over the city. A visit to the market of the Boquería at the heart of the Ramblas will illustrate, better than anything I could write, the reliability of statistics claiming that the Barcelonese spend more on eating than anybody else in Spain. This is especially true of the amount they spend on ingredients, with which they are familiar in the minutest detail.

It was in the shops of Barcelona that I learned about Catalonia's extensive repertoire of *charcuterie*. I discovered how to distinguish between *fuet* which are long, thin sausages made entirely with dried, uncooked meat, and *botifarras*, puddings which can be black, white, sweet or salty, and are even made with egg at certain times of the year. In the south of Catalonia, they spice their *charcuterie* with cumin and cinnamon, whereas in the north, particularly near Aragón, they only season with salt, pepper and occasionally garlic.

I discovered, too, that the Catalonians marry their region's red wines, especially those with great character and body such as those from Lérida, Penedés, and Priorato, with cheeses like Tupi, fermented with *eau-de-vie* high in the Pyrenees, the delicious *fromage de Serrat* from Lérida, the goat's milk *mato*, and *recuit*, a soft, set cheese made with ewes' milk which is ambrosial with honey.

Whilst in Barcelona, I recommend that you visit the Sagrada Familia, look at the shoe shops and a few art galleries and, to bring light relief to your ambling, that you indulge in some hot *buñuelos*, delicious doughnuts bought from a street-seller and eaten straight from their paper cones. To this, I would also add a wine tasting in one of the specialist shops of the city. Catalonia probably produces a greater variety of wines than any other region in the world. There is a wide range of red, white and *rosado* wines both young and aged from Alella, Penedés, Ampurdán or Costas del Segre. There are dessert wines, red and white from Tarragona and Priorato and, most famous of all, Catalonia is the home of Cava, the traditional sparkling wines of Spain.

Springtime in the Pyrenees brings brilliant new colours to the mountains, contrasting starkly with the simple buildings left by Romanesque architecture on its march through the area. Filled with water from the melted snows, the trout rivers gurgle exuberantly. This is the time of year when the woods bear the first mushrooms. The Catalans are great mycologists, and when their region does not produce them, they are imported mainly from the Basque Country. In the Pyrenees, most restaurants prepare them in a *revuelto*, which is similar to scrambled eggs, in omelettes, or simply sautéd with a little garlic, the classic way of preparing them.

It was to be in a wealthy inland town in the province of Gerona that I suddenly understood the several culinary cultures of Catalonia: one belonging to the sea, one to the mountains and one to the inland areas. The common denominator is that they all require slow care and attention. Mountain food, I had found to be a school of cooking in its own right, but that of the coast to be more of a collection of interesting dishes.

Inland, sitting at a table in a wonderful restaurant called La Rana, everything began to make sense in a uniquely Catalan way. I was once again on a farmstead, but here a magnificent garden took the place of the other *masía's* vines. In it, a profusion of vegetable and salad crops was growing, tall and graceful, just waiting to be picked. Amongst all this, was a myriad of the aromatic herbs so dear to all Mediterranean cooking. Outside, behind the dining-room, stood an open chimney that promised aromas of the sea, of grilling and of evocative smoke. The banquet began just a few minutes after we had taken our seats with a rich selection of local specialities, Serrano ham and *fuet*. Banquet is the only way I can describe the meal our host set before us.

Next came the salads. Whilst I was relishing the simple tomato and onion salad, the waiter was dressing an *exqueixada* of strips of transparent white cod, fresh and juicy tomatoes, onions and olives, with olive oil and vinegar.

Of all the many entrées, the *escalivada*, or roast vegetable salad, wore the crown. From the window overlooking the patio we had been watching one of the cooks poised beside the chimney's hood diligently roasting all sorts of vegetables that he selected from a large basket. All over Spain there is a deep-rooted tradition of cooking in the open air. In Catalonia, though, roasting vegetables over the embers of the fire is an art that is unique to this Mediterranean people. I was struck by how many different types of roasted vegetables were brought to our table. All the *escalivadas* I had eaten up until then consisted basically of skinned red peppers and aubergines, but this one also included tiny artichokes and the very sweetest of onions, still firm enough inside for their full flavour to be enjoyed yet almost caramelized on the outside. The flavour of these onions reminded me of a festival called La Calçotada, held in southern Catalonia, during which *calcots*, a kind of young spring onion, are roasted and eaten with the delicious Catalan *romesco* sauce.

Finally, but still part of the first course, a tray of cold boiled and dressed white beans, *empedrat*, arrived. As a lover of Asturian *fabadas* or bean stews, and of white beans cooked with clams, I wondered if I would like them as a cold salad. But like those that had preceded it, the flavour of this dish, with its whole yet tender beans, was peerless.

Then they brought us snails in a spicy sauce that were utterly delicious. All over Catalonia people love snails and cook them in a hundred and one ways – sometimes on their own, sometimes with other ingredients like peppers, onions and chilli, but the result is always tasty. Last of all came tiny grilled lamb cutlets. Unfortunately, having eaten far too much of everything, including the irresistible round bread or *pan de pueblo*, I was quite unable to manage dessert, although the most wonderful *crema catalana*, a caramelized egg custard, was a popular choice.

The Catalan people, and particularly those in rural inland areas, have not always eaten like this. There must be countless children of my parents' and even my older brother's generation who will have eaten Catalan hotpot, *escudella y carn d'olla*, 365 days a year. This is an important dish in Catalan cookery and is related to the *cocido* that has been made all over the Peninsula since time immemorial. In Catalonia, the dish uses a little pork, especially salt pork, with haricot beans or chick peas, carrots and leeks. When all the ingredients are well cooked, the *caldo*, or stock, is drained off and then used to make a soup with *pasta de lluvia*, raindrop pasta, or fine *fideos*, Spanish pasta. The vegetables are dressed with oil, and the meat is usually served with a good tomato sauce, creating three dishes in one.

As a Mediterranean area, most of Catalonia uses olive oil for cooking rather than pork fat, which is preferred inland and in mountain areas. Two of the four Denominations of Origin, or protected production areas, for Spanish olive oil are in Catalonia: Borjas Blancas in Lérida, and Siurana in Tarragona. Pork fat is used primarily for preserving meat products such as pork, duck or turkey. Catalan *confitat*, similar to many Basque meat preserves, is made by frying the selected meats in their own fat, then using the fat to cover the top of the ceramic pot in which the preserves are stored.

More than half of all Catalan dishes begin with a *sofrito* and end with a *picada*. *Sofrito* is chopped onions fried in olive oil until almost caramelized, then fried with a little tomato. *Picada* is a pounded sauce that can include pine kernels, almonds or hazelnuts, garlic, saffron and toasted bread, parsley, olive oil and even chocolate, depending on the nature of the dish. It serves a double purpose, both thickening and imparting new flavours to the dish. *All-i-oli* is a garlic and olive oil mayonnaise, now usually made with egg yolks, and delicious with all kinds of vegetables. *Sanfaina* is especially wonderful with poultry, which absorbs the flavours of the peppers, aubergines, garlic, tomato and herbs used to make the sauce.

Romesco is prepared as an accompaniment to meat, fish and even vegetable dishes. It is made from tiny, very hot *romesco* peppers, very different from the sweet *ñora* peppers, with almonds, tomatoes, garlic, fried bread, olive oil and a drop of sherry vinegar.

The word *romesco* takes me back to the years of my youth, and to the beach of Torredembarra in Tarragona province, where I spent two summers looking after children and saving up enough money to be able to afford a trip around France. The father of the family was Aurelio, a great amateur cook and a native of the Ebro delta area where they grow rice and make an exquisite dish called *romesco de peix*, an excellent fishermen's stew.

The *romesco de peix* that Aurelio would make on the days he managed to get to the fish auction consisted of several different fish and shellfish in a sauce, and its preparation follows the principles of the dishes made by the local fishermen. Aurelio first floured the pieces of *dentón*, one of the bream family, and monkfish, then fried them very briefly in hot oil. Once they had turned golden, he transferred them to a large earthenware *cazuela*. Next, he would prepare the *sofrito* and strain it on to the fish. Now was the time to prepare the sauce. He pounded almonds, peppers and a few garlic cloves, then stirred them into the *cazuela* for the final few minutes.

According to Aurelio, there are so many theories as to the origins of the dish that it is hard to believe any of them. Some say it was made by the Celts, who were early inhabitants of the region, or by Roman invaders. Others claim that it was the dish the Jaume I of Aragón declared, in 1232, to have been the best thing he had eaten in his life. The only fact we do know for certain is that peppers came to Catalonia in the sixteenth century!

In Catalonia, just as in Valencia, rice has always been an essential element in all celebrations. In fact, one particular dish, *arroz en cazuela de festa mayor*, actually means rice cooked in a *cazuela* on a feast day. Aurelio, however, always cooked his rice dishes in a *paella* and, if possible, in the open air. The family's favourite rice dish included saffron and fish stock as well as *dátiles de mar*, sea dates, molluscs which are very similar to ordinary mussels but which look just like a date. I can vividly remember the relish with which we devoured that wonderful, traditional feast.

GALICIA

Little about the beautiful Galician seaside village of Carnota has altered since I first went there at the end of the sixties. The sea still roars when it is angry, just as it does at Finisterre which looms in the distance like a great giant made of rock and moss. Now and again the roaring subsides and the sea languidly caresses mile upon mile of white sand. This is when the dolphins, looking for games, swim closer to the shore.

By contrast with so much of the Spanish coastline, the four provinces of this north-western corner of the Peninsula – La Coruña, Lugo, Orense and Pontevedra – have remained protected from international tourism and, to a certain extent, land speculation. There are no hotels and no restaurants in Carnota, just the village and the sea and a few summer residences of people from La Coruña and Madrid who come here to enjoy a dreamy holiday.

In Galicia, scents of sea and inland villages, of pine and eucalyptus, of seafood and corn bread hang in the air. It smells of tuna *empanada*, cheese, and *pulpo a feira*, octopus with olive oil and paprika; and its sounds are those of the *romería* or religious procession, and the drum.

Its cooking, whether in winter or summer, simple or dressed for the Carnival, makes the most of sea, mountains and valleys. What is the norm in Spanish cooking generally is more important than even in Galicia: quality ingredients and enjoyment in eating them. So too is the integrity of each dish. The old Galician saying that 'here, pork tastes like pork, fish tastes like fish, bread tastes like bread, and wine like wine' still holds true today.

Galician meat, the product of animals that graze in a green, peaceful world, is tender and of the very finest quality. On the butcher's counter there are black puddings, cooking *chorizos* and a few pieces of fresh or salt belly pork, and little else in summer. Meat is kept for winter days and the festivities which mark the beginning of Lent.

As the summer draws to a close, so come festivals celebrating the cities' and villages' saints' days, fairs and *romerías* and the great feasts with which these people traditionally follow such acts of devotion. I especially remember the festival of Saint Andrew, whose sanctuary is some 10 kilometres from the village of Teixedo, 150 metres above the Cantabrian sea and set in a startlingly beautiful landscape of open sea and almost uninhabited mountains.

Once the rituals have been performed, the crowd galvanizes itself for music, songs and food. There are two kinds of meal to be eaten. There are those produced by the experienced, for whom these expeditions are part of family tradition and who therefore bring everything with them, from canopies and tablecloths to locally made Sagardelos porcelain crockery. Or there are makeshift meals enjoyed by those who are perfectly happy to buy portions of octopus, *empanada* or roast meat from the stalls that accompany such events.

The tablecloths spread over the grass display full and varied menus that reveal the areas from which the families have come. The people from the coast will have cooked seafood, particularly their favourite *nécoras* (one of the crab family), and fish *empanadas*, whilst the people from the countryside will have brought one of their own chickens, plus lamb or rabbit, roast with garlic or in a pie. Wine will be flowing everywhere. For dessert, there will be almond tarts and home-made egg and milk flan followed by *aguardiente* or *eau-de-vie* made from *orujo*, the residue from pressing grapes, or herbs of which the men are so fond. The variety and quality of the food shows that although this is a poor region it produces the most exquisite gifts from both land and sea.

One of the cornerstones of Galician gastronomy is shell-fish. Nearly all species are eaten simply boiled in soft water, but my sister-in-law, who is a Galician and is wise in these matters, insists that they should be cooked in seawater. In this part of the world, seafood is eaten as an appetizer or as a first course, usually accompanied by mayonnaise or vinaigrette. You can tell that it must be no rare indulgence here by the relish with which people make short work of it and the expertise with which they dispatch the shells.

Of the crustaceans with large, strong shells, the *buey*, a large crab, has huge pincers and a smooth shell, whilst the spider crab, *centolla*, is not only more beautiful but finer-tasting too. The heavier they are the better, as this means there is more meat on them. *Langostas* and *bogavantes*, spiny lobsters and lobsters, are served simply boiled with nothing more than a bay leaf. Then their tail is parted from the great armour protecting their body. According to custom, the tail is the part that is most appreciated, but a Galician will savour the furthest reaches of each claw.

It was in the Rías Bajas that I learned to eat clams raw, and cockles, limpets and oysters without lemon. The Rías Bajas also taught me how to cook octopus and showed me the delights of poached turbot dressed with a simple *ajada* of oil, paprika and fried onion. *Ajada* is a traditional dressing used by the Galicians on potatoes, vegetables and many of their fish dishes.

Although it is not the only star of Galician festivities, no celebration would be complete without octopus. After beating it in the time-honoured way to tenderize it and bring out its flavour, it is boiled, then left in the hot water to soften. I like it best *a la gallega*, with potatoes and onions, but the most popular way of preparing it is *a feira*, festive style, simply cutting it into pieces, sprinkling it with olive oil and paprika and serving it on the old-fashioned wooden plates that you will find in Galicia's local markets and bars.

Another great speciality is the Galician *empanada*, which I think is the best dough-based dish made in Spain. It comes in many forms: I have eaten round and square ones, simple and complex ones, rich and light ones. Some are made with bread dough using wheat flour, and used to be cooked in the local baker's oven, while others have a dough made of maize and a little rye flour.

The secret of the *empanada* is in the *comparga* or filling. Common to the majority is a tomato and onion *sofrito* with garlic, paprika, or better still saffron, ham and the ubiquitous dash of wine. Other ingredients are variable and can include sardines, mussels, eel, white tuna and salt cod. Lamprey, which has been deliciously encased in a luxurious puff pastry, is also used, but only on special occasions.

No excursion is made, no day spent at the beach, nor festivity or *romería* organized without *empanadas*. No restaurant or bar is without it, and on board the great fishing vessels, which for a long time counted Galician cooks among their crews, it is very much part of the diet.

With the onset of winter, meat and other substantial dishes become more popular. This is especially true inland where cold and damp are the only constants of the changeable climate that reigns over the region. From November to January, the indisputable symbol of the countryman's wealth, the pig, is slaughtered. These same months see a few joints of veal and lamb roasted, and partridges casseroled – preferably red-footed ones for, according to the people of Lugo, they are far better than the black-footed birds. Towards early spring, quail will appear on the menu, and wild boar is plentiful in the mountains, although you will seldom come across it in local restaurants.

In people's homes, whatever meats are available are boiled, and the results used to make *caldo* by adding potatoes, greens, beans and a little pork fat. The best and most traditional *caldos* are based on a stock of veal, smoked or salted pork hock and boiling hen. My favourite of all the varieties is the one that is made with turnip tops or *navizas*, young turnip leaves. Pork fat is used in everything.

Carnival is the time for another quintessentially Galician dish, *lacón con grelos*, pork with turnip leaves. Carnival has always been a time of great feasts in which pork has featured heavily, almost as if people felt a need to store up energy prior to the period of fasting which would follow.

It was at this season that I last visited Santiago de Compostela, an enchanting and beautiful university city and religious centre which still has a light-hearted spirit, despite the fact that it rains constantly. The city has one of Europe's most fascinating markets which still has a village feel to it in spite of the city's important past. I have often asked myself whether it is the flowers they sell at the main entrance which draw me back again and again, or the conversation I always strike up with the village women who, sitting behind huge wicker baskets, are able to sell me anything they want simply because my will is no match for their rhetoric. The softness with which the Galicians speak Castilian is as remarkable as their tenacity as salespeople. I could not tell you how many cheeses I have been lulled into buying in the square behind the main market by the voices of fifty or sixty women calling out, 'The best cheese in the land', or 'Buy this one *rapaciña* (darling), it is really good.'

Their persuasiveness also meant that I have often caught the plane back home loaded down with kilos of *pimientos del Padrón*, a type of small pepper from the village of Padrón in Pontevedra which I call 'Russian roulette peppers'. Deep green in colour and smaller than your little finger, they can be either sweet or terribly hot, depending on the time of the year. But they are unpredictable too; within a batch some will be hot but not others. The village women in Santiago sell them by the hundred, counting them out two by two into modern plastic bags.

The cheeses in the market are similar to one another in style although each has its own individual character. They are made with cows' milk, as are all Galician cheeses. They are fresh and young, round and flat; the exception being the well-known *tetilla*, meaning breast, whose shape needs no explanation, and San Simón, which is conical. These soft, creamy and mild cheeses are made in many households in the hamlets and villages of Galicia, by expert men and women. I have heard a local saying that 'cheese tastes like kisses, and this is the taste of the people of Galicia'.

I would recommend that, if given the chance, you try the San Simón which is made in Lugo, and is smoked over shavings of birch bark which gives it its characteristic orange colour. The *tetilla* is also delicious, as is *Ulloa*, a similar tasting but flat-shaped cheese.

Apart from *filloas*, lace pancakes, desserts do not take up many pages in the catalogue of Galician gastronomy. Now and again, though, you will drool over amazing puff pastries filled with *cabello de angel*, which are sweetened pumpkin threads, or a piece of the famous *tarta de Santiago* made of eggs, almonds, sugar and fine breadcrumbs, dusted with icing sugar and imprinted with a cross of Saint James on top by means of two etched metal plates. I can also whole-heartedly recommend the chestnuts from Orense, both in syrup and glacé, and the cherries in *orujo* – all are exquisite.

I could not leave Galicia without mentioning its wines and *aguardiente*, or *eau-de-vie*. They are an intrinsic part of many local ceremonies.

The Albariño vine was apparently brought to Galicia either by Benedictine monks from Cluny or by Cistercian monks from the Rhine and the Moselle in the twelfth century and they are now grown and made into wonderful wines in the Salnés Valley in Pontevedra. When it is well made, I think it is one of the most exquisite white wines we have in Spain. I should warn you, however, that it has not always been made as it should be. I have tasted two- and even three-year-old Albariños, and very interesting they have been, but the best have always been the very new ones which are lively, deeply aromatic, characterful but not too acidic.

In the Rosal district near the border with Portugal, Albariño grapes are sometimes blended with small quantities of other grape varieties such as Treixadura and Caiño to produce a wine that I recommend drinking with the superb Atlantic fish that are to be found in the restaurants in these parts.

Red and white wines are made and drunk in every corner of Galicia, but it is the district of Ribadavia in Orense that produces the lion's share of the harvest: the Ribeiro wine. For my taste, the best is the white, even the wine that is sold unfiltered in some of the *tascas*, or rough-and-ready local bars. The red wines from here and from Valdeorras, which are in fact almost purple, give of their best when married with the local foods.

Aguardiente, just like wine and cheese, is intrinsic to the life of the Galicians. Men drink it first thing in the morning to galvanize their energies for the day's work. There are many variations on the *aguardiente* theme, but the best I have had were at a restaurant called Villas in Santiago. There were four kinds of *aguardiente* on offer there: white, *tostado* or toasted, apple and peach – all served in tiny, very chilled glasses. *Aguardiente* is used for the *queimada*, a dramatic and ancient night-time ceremony. The spirit is heated in a great china pot with sugar and a zest of lemon, then set alight. Ceremony or no, I have always thought it is a great shame for the *aguardiente* to go up in flames.

THE BASQUE COUNTRY AND NAVARRA

Night is drawing in over the Cantabrian sea and the boats that set sail from Fuenterrabía at dawn in search of the prized hake are safely back in the harbour, at rest. A Basque fisherman with a pipe clenched between his teeth is loading a few sea bream, fresh from the water and glistening metallically pink, into a wooden box. The net maker and repairer, her labours over for the day, makes ready to go home. She picks up a wicker basket full of tiny anchovies that is a much appreciated gift from a fellow townsman.

To the south, the autumnal moss greens and ochres that cover the mountain and the valley contrast with the last glimmers of the fading sun on the sea. Apples hang in the trees and the thoughts of the *casero*, the local farmer, turn to cider.

One side of my family is from the Basque Country, which is the region bounded by the Cantabrian sea and the French Basque Pyrenees to the north, Castile to the south, and Aragón and Cantabria to the east and west. My grandmother, who was born in Estella, argued that there were not three Basque provinces, as the politicians maintain, but four: Vizcaya, Guipúzcoa, Alava and her beloved Navarra.

The general consensus among Spaniards is that here is where one will eat the best food in Spain. The Basques are tremendously demanding when they shop for food, for they are keen cooks and love eating well. Here, women compete with men, and everyone competes with the professional chefs, resulting in dishes of a quality and variety almost unequalled anywhere else in Spain. There is, in fact, more to Basque cooking than is often supposed: it is far more than a motley collection of recipes. It is the cooking of a people who have fought, danced and drunk cider hidden away in the mountains and valleys of the Pyrenees since prehistory. Anyone seeking to unravel the origins of Europe will find that the Basques hold many of the secrets that have still to be revealed. Little is known, for example, about how food was prepared in prehistoric times, yet traces of those ancient ways may still be present in today's cooking – it is a fascinating subject.

Cooking here was hardly affected by the Roman and Moorish invasions, unlike Spain's other culinary traditions. It was, however, influenced by the pilgrims on their way to Santiago, who passed through the Basque Country carrying flavours of Europe, and by its geographical position as a Pyrenean threshold between Africa and Europe. It has come down to us today with certain additional touches, relics of the British presence in Laburdi and Zuberoa, on the French side of the Pyrenees, for over 300 years, and of the important trading relationship that existed between England's south coast ports and Bilbao.

Another strong influence was the number of famous chefs who crossed the border from France into the Basque Country, especially to San Sebastián, during the nineteenth century. The more austere style of the neighbouring Castilian cooking is also responsible for some features of the Basque style.

A day in the life of a Basque kitchen begins with a visit to the market. Be it La Brecha in San Sebastián, the central market in Bilbao or the one and only market in Ordicia, there is little to choose between them as far as the high quality of the food they sell is concerned. The selection of vegetables that the country women bring down from their hamlets every day is an absolute delight. In the springtime everything is new-born and tender, especially the tiny peas, broad beans and carrots. There will be newly sprouted dwarf spinach, tied together in bundles with coloured ribbon, artichokes from Navarra and green and white asparagus. They also bring sacks of the black beans that revolutionized the rural diet when they were introduced in the sixteenth century.

Under the covered part of the market some country women set out their sacks on the ground whilst others unfold their typical red and white check cloths on high wooden tables, laying upon them glassware, cakes, chocolate *bizcochos*, jars of honey and cheese made either by themselves or by a local shepherd There are ewes' milk cheeses from the Aralar mountains or from Idiazábal some smoked, others not, some young, others mature – and breads made from maize flour as well as from wheat.

One of the most famous Basque recipes, the *menestra*, comes to the family table and to restaurant menus with the advent of the new spring vegetables. This dish brings together several kinds of vegetable – artichokes, chard leaves, fresh peas, green haricot beans and asparagus – that have all been cooked separately but are served dressed with a stock made from olive oil, garlic, wine and flour. Those that are made in Tudela are the most famous, for the town's gardens grow small delectable artichokes, tiny lettuce hearts, asparagus and peppers. Mushrooms are another of the Basques' great loves, all year round.

Fish is the Basques' favourite food and the most fundamental ingredient in so many of its recipes. Over three-quarters of recipes cooked in Euskadi are made with seafood for, above everything else, the Basques are a seafaring people who love the sea, particularly the Atlantic which they have crossed throughout their history, sometimes in search of fish, sometimes in search of fortune, work or adventure.

Once I nearly fell in love with a handsome fisherman in the Vizcayan port of Ondárroa simply because of the *marmitako* he gave me to eat. A festival was being celebrated on the beach and the men were competing against each other to see who could make the best stew. My fisherman, however, told me that these 'landlubbers' *marmitakos*', as he called them, had no taste of the sea and bore little resemblance to those he made on board his tuna-fishing boat in a little stove just large enough to accommodate the *marmita* pot.

Ever since that day, I have been enamoured of the fish dishes that these people make with the delicacies from the sea. Tuna is delicious in the summer, especially *a la plancha*, cooked on a grill. Superb salads are made with fillets of white-fleshed *albacora*, also from the tuna family. However, the fish that is most talked about, and on which the Basques will spend most money, is hake. My Basque friends assure me, and I know this to be true myself, that the very best hake is that which is caught on a hook and line, not far off the Basque coastline. These fish are brightly coloured, their skins shot with reflections of silver and iridescence that create a most beautiful effect.

The local people can distinguish at a glance between these fish and the hake that, whilst also fresh, are in effect chilled, having been caught by dragnets in the fishing grounds of the Gran Sol and off the coast of Morocco. Hake is a very delicate fish, and when it is caught in large nets it suffocates without fighting, thereby deteriorating. This does not happen to the fish that is caught on the line as it is hauled out of the water immediately it takes the hook. When these hake are unloaded in Fuenterrabía they are so fresh that they have to rest for several hours before being cooked so that their flesh loses some of its rigidity. The best I have ever eaten was in a restaurant in Ondárroa. All the chef did was to put the hake on the steel hotplate of a magnificent wood-fired range with a little salt and a few drops of olive oil.

Basque cooking has a recipe for any fish you can name. It has even managed to turn apparently unattractive fish into well-known delicacies. I am referring to *bacalao* or salt cod, which is delicious *al pil-pil*, cooked in an emulsion of oil and garlic, or *a la vizcaína* with dried peppers and onions. Cod fishing has been an important chapter in the life of a people whose economy in times gone by depended to a large extent on the success of its exploits in the cold waters off the coast of Canada.

The Basque culinary repertoire includes numerous sauces, especially for fish, and they are the great speciality of the men who take refuge in the Gastronomic Societies that were created in the nineteenth century in San Sebastián. There, alone or with friends, they will cook to give pleasure to themselves or to others. These men know only a few recipes, but they cook these with such dedication that they attain almost professional standards. Most of the societies only allow women as guests of their members, and then only at lunch-time and never on Fridays. This is when the men are out to celebrate, and they will eventually be found dining on a succulent *cazuela* of hake in green sauce, drinking Txakolí, a local wine, or a good Rioja Reserva, and singing as only Basque men do.

Until a relatively short time ago, women were not allowed

into the cider houses of Guipúzcoa either when they opened their doors for the traditional cider-tasting in January each year. Cider houses usually comprise two large rooms. The first is generally both kitchen and dining-room, with tables but no chairs, as the idea is to go back and forth between this room and the other where twelve or thirteen vats, or *kupekaks*, of cider await the moment of truth. Customers pay for the right to drink as much cider and eat as much as they can while strolling about with their friends.

In farmhouses, or *caseríos*, in the mountains and valleys, particularly in Alava where Basque cooking has very distinctive features, seafood no longer dominates. These *caseríos* are slowly dying, suffocated by industrialization and progress, but left behind is a marvellous legacy of exceptionally good meat and stew recipes. One such superb dish is a red pinto bean stew which often provides both lunch and supper for many Basque country labourers every day of the year. At the same time, out of this disappearing way of life, a new breed of *caseríos* is emerging. Local people are perpetuating culinary traditions by opening restaurants where you can sample dishes that would otherwise have been lost to time.

There you will find one of my favourites, *piperrada*, which reminds me of days I spent in the Navarran Pyrenees. It consists of garlic, onion, red peppers, tomatoes and fresh herbs served with a good slice of ham. I would also recommend roast leg of lamb with *pochas*, fresh white shelled beans; wild autumn mushrooms simply but beautifully sautéd; and, most especially, game dishes such as hare with walnut sauce. Apples, walnuts, red and white wine, onion, garlic and chocolate are some of the principal ingredients that give this dish an exquisitely original flavour.

A tour of this region and its cooking would be incomplete without a look at the *Euskal Sukaldaritza Berria*, or New

Basque Cookery. In the late 1970s, new winds blew across the kitchen ranges of a group of professional Basque chefs. Determined to maintain the excellence of their cooking and the quality of the ingredients that had always been its foundation, they began to create new recipes and adapt old ones following a series of basic principles, principles that were also rocking the foundations of culinary tradition across Europe, even in France. The most relevant were shorter cooking times for vegetables, fish and meat; the use of vegetable in preference to animal fats; and special care in presentation. The new Basque cookery also placed great emphasis on the preparation of delicious desserts, so lacking in the Peninsula's culinary repertoire as a whole, and on the local cheeses and wines, especially Rioja and Txakolí.

For me, however, the greatest success of current Basque cooking – not necessarily just the new style – stems from the professional Basque chef's love of age-old dishes. He makes them taste sublime, and as a result of careful study has managed to single out the very best and leave behind those of little real interest. These chefs have had an extraordinary influence on cooking all over Spain. They have given a completely new look and flavour to traditional fish recipes, introduced the best quality olive oils and mellow cider vinegars, moderated the use of garlic, lightened sauces and emphasized precise timing of pasta and rice cooking.

It was at the table of one of these chefs that I first tasted well-made Txakolí. I had for years been drinking the wines that are served under this name in bars all over the Basque Country, especially in the *asadores* which specialize in roast fish and meat. They were young wines with a little sharpness, very similar to Portuguese Vinho Verde.

In Guetaria, a fishing village where one of the prettiest vineyards in the land nudges the sea, Pedro Chueca, the master of Txakolí, now produces a wine that is the perfect companion to most of the dishes in the Basque repertoire – dishes which marry equally well with one of Spain's best red wines from Rioja. Part of the Basque province of Alava makes a major contribution to the wine region of Rioja. Together with Txakolí and Rioja, the Basques are also very partial to the *rosados* and matured reds from Navarra. What more perfect match could you wish for?

APPETIZERS
Tapas

The word *tapa* translates literally as a lid. *Tapas*, or small portions of food served in Spanish bars, are widely believed to have evolved from the nineteenth-century Andalusian custom of bar owners presenting customers with a slice of ham or sausage covering their glass of sherry. As this became a tradition, so the number of appetizers increased and it was a short step to the many *tapas* available to us today. But *tapas* are most emphatically not 'fast food' Iberian-style. Their secret is that of all good Spanish food: quality and freshness of ingredients.

Nowadays, the majority of *tapas* bars, from the most humble to the most sophisticated, offer a varied display of dishes which range from the conventional to the inspired. According to your appetite, you can eat just a few as a prelude to lunch or dinner, or you can indulge in several portions, or *raciones*, so that the *tapas* will suffice as a main meal. Often, the cook's whims of the day will be casually chalked up on a blackboard. On the other hand, you might find yourself in a bar that appears not to serve *tapas*, but on venturing to ask, you will be delivered a forty- or fifty-line litany of all your hungry imagination could wish to savour. If this happens you would almost certainly be in Andalusia, the home of *tapas*.

But *tapas* go beyond cookery – they are a way of life. The Engish equivalent of the verb *tapear* would be something like bar-hopping: eating little snacks as you go; although this conveys nothing of the fun, sights and smells that are an integral part of the whole experience.

I had to wait until I was almost thirty, and in the company of a group of English friends, to discover what *tapas* were all about in the wider sense. We had booked a table for nine o'clock at a restaurant in Seville called 'La Dorada', which serves the most marvellous fish, and we decided to go for a walk around the Triana area first. We crossed the Guadalquivir river, over the bridge that is named after the Triana, to the city's left bank, and slipped down the narrow streets towards the heart of this most fascinating part of the town. Triana was throbbing with life – in its streets, its grand restaurants and its tiny bars. All we did was submerge outselves in its world, and eat and drink just as its people do, making our way little by little through lots of different dishes – roast green peppers, mushrooms with garlic, fried whitebait, *tortilla* and *chipirones*, delicious tiny squid. We alternated between beer, Fino and Manzanilla sherries, always served cold and in their correct glasses. We were late arriving at the restaurant but it did not matter; there was no hurry.

Ⓥ COLD TOMATO AND PEPPER SOUP
Salmorejo

Although this recipe ought really to have been included in the chapter on soups, it is also served as a *tapa* in some of the bars of Andalusia and Madrid, where they tend to produce more refined renditions. When I think of *salmorejo*, I recall a memorable lunch in the Santa Lucía olive oil factory in Baena in Córdoba province, where the Núñez de Prado brothers produce a delicious virgin olive oil. The lady of the house, who loves cooking, makes a *salmorejo* that is almost impossible to match. So far she has refused to let me have the secret, but I think the problem is that I will never learn to pound the way she does.

SERVES 4

450 g (1 lb) breadcrumbs, mostened with water and well drained

250 ml (8 fl oz) olive oil

250 g (9 oz) ripe tomatoes, skinned, de-seeded and coarsely chopped

250 g (9 oz) green peppers, de-seeded and finely chopped

3 garlic cloves, peeled

1 teaspoon sherry vinegar

Salt

For the garnish

1 tablespoon olive oil

1 slice bread, diced

1 hard-boiled egg, chopped

25 g (1 oz) Serrano ham or dry-cured ham, chopped (optional)

Place all the soup ingredients in a food processor and blend until smooth. As this dish contain no water, it should be much thicker than a *gazpacho*. Place in a bowl and refrigerate until ready to serve. Just before serving, heat the oil and fry the bread until crisp and brown, then use to garnish the soup with the egg and ham.

Ⓥ MARINATED OLIVES
Aceitunas Aliñadas

It was in the Triana market in Seville, now lost due to excavations, that I understood the importance of the *aliño*, or marinade, in Andalusia. The following recipe is a delicious version of the traditional dish, although that, of course, uses fresh olives, which are impossible to buy outside the countries in which they are harvested. In its natural state, the olive, whether green or purple, is a very bitter fruit, which is why the Andalusians give them a gentle pounding then leave them to soak for 3 days, changing the water frequently until they lose some of their bitterness. Then they are put into a marinade of garlic, herbs and spices which transforms them into an unequalled appetizer.

SERVES 4

225 g (8 oz) green or black olives

1/2 teaspoon ground cumin

1/2 teaspoon chopped fresh oregano

1/2 teaspoon crushed fresh rosemary

1/2 teaspoon chopped fresh thyme

1/2 teaspoon fennel seeds

2 bay leaves

4 garlic cloves, peeled and crushed

4 tablespoons sherry vinegar

Pack the olives into a screw-top jar just large enough to hold them. Mix all the other ingredients together and pour over the olives. Top up with water, if necessary. Screw on the lid, shake well, and leave to marinate at room temperature for 3–4 days.

Ⓥ ALL-I-OLI POTATOES
Patatas All-i-oli

The extensive repertoire of *tapas* dishes includes many recipes for potatoes. This is one of those I make most frequently in the summer when I have time to use the barbecue to cook the meat and fish for which this is the perfect accompaniment. If you would rather use less garlic, however, this sauce is not for you; so you may prefer my other favourite, the famous Aliñadas dressed potatoes from Huelva. For this delicious recipe, simply boil the potatoes and toss them in a mixture of fresh, very finely chopped spring onion, freshly chopped parsley, virgin olive oil, 2 peeled and crushed garlic cloves and a teaspoon of sherry vinegar.

In bars, *patatas all-i-oli* are usually served with a sauce made from egg, which makes it lighter. Once the potatoes are mixed into the sauce, parsley is snipped over the top.

SERVES 6–8

4 garlic cloves, peeled
Salt
150 ml (5 fl oz) olive oil
A few drops of water
Juice of ½ lemon

450 g (1 lb) new potatoes,
  peeled, boiled and diced
1 tablespoon chopped fresh
  parsley to serve

Use a pestle and mortar to crush the garlic to a fine paste, then season with salt. Add the oil slowly but steadily – a traditional oil dispenser is perfect for this – stirring continuously until the sauce thickens. Mix a few drops of water and lemon juice into the sauce to taste. Mix the potatoes with the sauce, sprinkle with parsley and serve.

BREAD WITH TOPPINGS
Hogazas

In Castile, *hogaza* is a round bread with a hard crust and a spongy texture, and a *pincho* is a piece of bread with something on top. At the counter of the bar L'Herranz on Calle Echegarai in Madrid, you can sample a number of variations inspired by the delicious, famous Catalan *pincho, pan amb tomaquet* or bread and tomato. My favourite *hogazas* are ham and tomato, peppers and anchovies, and red peppers with salt cod. The Serrano ham *hogaza*, better known as *pan con tomate y jamón*, has no other secrets than good quality ham. *Hogazas* could not be easier to make. The bread is cut into thick slices, each slice is cut in two and spread with fresh tomato sauce and topped with the chosen ingredients before serving.

SERVES 4

4 thick slices round farmhouse bread

For the tomato sauce

500 g (1 lb 2 oz) ripe tomatoes, skinned, de-seeded and crushed

3 tablespoons virgin olive oil

1 garlic clove, peeled and crushed

A few cumin seeds

For the tomato and ham topping

4 slices Serrano ham or dry-cured ham

For the pepper and anchovy topping

4 red peppers
Salt

1 × 50 g (2 oz) tin anchovies

For the pepper and salt cod topping

50 g (2 oz) dried salt cod,   *4 red peppers*
   cut into very fine strips   *Salt*

Cut the slices of bread in half. Mix together the tomato sauce ingredients and spread the bread liberally with the sauce.

For the tomato and ham *hogaza*, simply top the bread with slices of ham and serve.

For the pepper and anchovy topping, pre-heat the oven to 180°C/350°F/Gas 4. Roast the peppers for about 15 minutes, then remove the skins, de-seed them and leave them to cool. Season the peppers with salt, then cut them into thin strips. Top the bread with the tomato sauce, then the peppers and anchovies and serve.

For the pepper and salt cod topping, the strips of salt cod should be cut so finely that they are almost transparent. Soak them in cold water for a few hours, then drain them well. Prepare the peppers in the same way as for the previous topping. Spread the bread with the tomato sauce, then the peppers and salt cod strips and serve.

PRAWNS IN GARLIC
Gambas al Ajillo

In the heart of Old Madrid, in Cuchilleros Street, there is a little bar which has small earthenware dishes full of transparent prawns sitting in the window, ready to be cooked. I must admit that I have never eaten more delicious prawns in any sea port. When I make this recipe at home, I add a little chilli before cooking them; do try it if you like chilli.

SERVES 4

250 g (9 oz) uncooked prawns

2–3 tablespoons olive oil

2 garlic cloves, peeled and sliced

Salt

To peel the prawns, hold them by the tail and twist off the head, then gently peel away the shell and legs, leaving the tails intact.

Heat the oil in a small flameproof earthenware dish and add the prawns, garlic and salt. Cook for 2–3 minutes and serve still sizzling.

Prawns with Overcoats
Gambas con Gabardina

The word *gabardina* means raincoat and, in the same way as the flour protects fried fish, so the beer batter seals the delicate prawn allowing it to cook in its own juice. Prawns make such wonderful starters to a meal because they are so delicious, yet so light, whetting the appetite for what is to follow.

SERVES 4

500 g (1 lb 2 oz) uncooked
   king prawns
200 g (7 oz) plain flour
A pinch of salt

475 ml (16 fl oz) light ale
8 strands saffron
Olive oil for frying

To peel the prawns, hold them by the tail and twist off the head, then gently peel away the legs and the rest of the shell, leaving the last part of the shell and the tail.

Mix together the flour, salt and light ale. Crush the saffron, then dissolve it in a little boiling water. Mix it into the flour and ale to form a smooth, fairly thick, batter the consistency of béchamel or white sauce. Dry the prawns on a clean cloth, pick them up by the tail. Heat the oil and fry a few prawns at a time. Once the prawns are cooked, drain off the excess oil and serve immediately.

BAKED SCALLOPS
Vieiras al Horno

Some fishmongers sell fresh scallops already opened and cleaned, which can save your preparation time, but do make sure they are plump and firm. It is important that the bread is not noticed, so the crumbs must be very fine, almost transparent, and made from brown bread. Sometimes scallops are simply cooked on their shells, *a la plancha*, with a little chopped onion, parsley and white wine.

SERVES 4

4 scallops, scrubbed
2 tablespoons olive oil
50 g (2 oz) Spanish onions, peeled and finely chopped
2 small garlic cloves, peeled and crushed
25 g (1 oz) very fine fresh brown breadcrumbs

2 teaspoons chopped fresh parsley
Salt and freshly ground black pepper
A pinch of freshly grated nutmeg
1 lemon, cut into wedges, to serve

Pre-heat the oven to 180°C/350°F/Gas 4.

Cut through the hinge of the scallop shell and take off the rounded shell. Scrape off the beard-like fringe from around the scallop and remove the black intestinal thread. Slide a sharp knife under the scallop and remove both scallop and coral from the shell. Clean the shells thoroughly.

Heat the oil and fry the onions and garlic until transparent. Remove from the heat, add the scallops, breadcrumbs and parsley and season to taste with salt, freshly ground black pepper and a little nutmeg. Fill the shells with the mixture. Bake for 10 minutes and serve with the lemon wedges.

FRIED COD STICKS
Soldaditos de Pavía

This is Seville's classic *tapa*. Angel Muro's excellent book, *El Practicón*, gives this recommendation: 'Take good long strips of salt cod, soaked, cleared of skin and scales, coated in batter coloured with a touch of saffron, and fry in plenty of oil. They should be well browned and crispy.' Delicious.

SERVES 4

250 g (9 oz) dried salt cod
Juice of 1 lemon
75 g (3 oz) plain flour
1½ teaspoons baking
    powder
A pinch of salt

3 strands of saffron
50 ml (2 fl oz) water
50 ml (2 fl oz) milk
3 tablespoons olive oil
Olive oil for frying

Soak the cod in water at room temperature for 24–36 hours, depending on the thickness of the pieces, changing the water at least 3 times. Drain the fish thoroughly and remove the membrane, skin and bones. Cut the cod into strips 5 cm (2 in) long and 1 cm (½ in) wide and sprinkle with lemon juice.

To make the batter, mix the flour, baking powder and salt. Lightly roast the saffron for a few seconds in a dry pan over a moderate heat then crush it and add it to the flour. Stir in the water, milk and oil and mix until smooth. Heat at least 1 cm (½ in) of oil in a frying-pan. Dip the cod pieces in the batter and fry until golden-brown and crispy on both sides. Drain off the excess oil on kitchen paper and serve immediately.

MIXED FRIED FISH
Fritura de Pescado

Mention fried fish to me and I think of Cádiz and the paper cones you buy from the *freidurías*, the fried food shops, that face on to the streets. These were not invented by the Andalusians but by the Galicians who emigrated south in search of the sun and who applied their artistry with the frying-pan to the amazing variety of fish that is brought into this city from the Atlantic. Sea salt, strong flour and olive oil from Córdoba or Jaén are the only other requirements. It is said in these parts that the British tradition of fish and chips was introduced to those islands by the sherry traders from the city of Cádiz.

SERVES 4

175 g (6 oz) small red mullet
Salt
175 g (6 oz) large squid
175 g (6 oz) haddock fillet, cut into small pieces

75 g (3 oz) plain flour
Olive oil for deep-frying
1 lemon, cut into wedges, to serve

Holding the mullet by the tail, scrape away the scales from the tail to the head using the blunt side of a knife. Slit along the belly of the fish and remove the guts. Wash the fish under cold running water and rub the inside with a little salt to clean it. Cut off the head just below the gills, slice off the tail and cut off the fins with scissors.

To prepare the squid, pull the head and tentacles away from the body. Pull off and discard the skin (1). Cut the tentacles from the head just above the eye. Discard the head

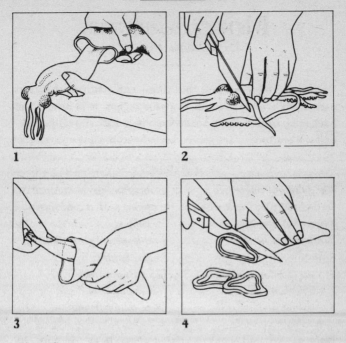

and cut off the beak (2). Wash the body and tentacles thoroughly in running water and remove and discard the transparent bony section (3). Drain and cut the body into rings (4).

Dust all the fish in the flour and shake in a sieve to remove the surplus. Heat the oil in a deep-fryer and fry the fish separately for 4–5 minutes each. Drain off the excess oil on kitchen paper, garnish with lemon wedges and serve immediately.

FISH CROQUETTES
Croquetas

I like fish croquettes best, but those made with poultry and ham come a close second. For this recipe, it is best if the béchamel sauce is light, made from half milk and half stock, and the croquettes are served straight from the pan.

SERVES 4

400 g (14 oz) white fish
500 ml (17 fl oz) water
Juice of ½ lemon
Fresh dill to taste
Salt
375 ml (13 fl oz) milk
2 tablespoons olive oil

½ medium-sized Spanish
    onion, peeled and finely
    chopped
3 tablespoons plain flour
2 eggs, beaten
175 g (6 oz) fresh
    breadcrumbs
Olive oil for frying

Place the fish and water in a fish kettle or large pan with the lemon, dill and a little salt. Bring to the boil, cover and poach gently for 7–10 minutes until the fish is cooked. Drain, skin and flake the fish, reserving the stock. Combine the milk and stock to make 750 ml (1¼ pints).

Heat the oil in a deep pan and fry the onion until transparent. Add the flour and brown for 1–2 minutes, remove from the heat and leave to cool. Still off the heat, add half the stock mixture little by little to avoid lumps. Return to the heat and add the rest of the mixture. Cook for another 10 minutes or until it does not taste floury and then add the fish. Pour the mixture into a bowl, cool, then refrigerate for 2–3 hours.

To prepare the croquettes for frying, shape small portions of the paste into balls and dip them first into the beaten egg, then into the breadcrumbs. The croquettes can be deep-fried or fried in plenty of hot oil until golden-brown. Drain off the excess oil on kitchen paper.

SALT COD WITH DRIED RED PEPPERS AND OLIVE OIL
Pericana

I remember the chef at a restaurant in Alicante making *pericana*. The salt cod was relatively thin, so he followed the fast method of de-salting it: grilling the pieces of fish over hot coals or a hotplate for about 3 minutes to soften them, thus making it easy to remove the skin and bones. Next he soaked the cod in water for 2–3 hours. Serve with crusty bread.

SERVES 4

250 g (9 oz) dried salt cod, cut into very thin pieces
150 ml (5 fl oz) olive oil

2–3 dried red choricero peppers
6 garlic cloves, peeled and finely chopped

Grill the cod for about 3 minutes to soften it, then remove the skin and bones. Soak the cod in water for 2 or 3 hours.

Heat the oil, remove from the heat and blanch the peppers for a few seconds in the hot oil, taking care that they do not burn. The peppers will go brittle. Remove from the oil, discard the stem and seeds and put to one side. Pour the oil out of the pan and sweat the cod and garlic for about 10 minutes until cooked. Finely flake the fish, discarding the skin and bones. Crumble the fried peppers and mix them into the cod with the garlic. Pour over the oil to taste and mix well.

BURGOS BLACK PUDDING OR CHORIZO PINCHOS
Pinchos de Morcilla de Burgos o de Chorizo

It will not be easy, outside Spain, to find the rice and onion black puddings that are made in the area around Burgos, but if you are travelling in Spain I suggest you try them so that you understand my insistence on using them. However, this recipe can be made with black pudding from anywhere and still tastes wonderful. The very thin spicy *chistorra* sausages from Navarra are ideal for *chorizo pinchos*, but any of the many other kinds of this spicy sausage also taste good.

SERVES 4

2 tablespoons olive oil
4 thick pieces Spanish black
  pudding or spicy sausage

4 thick slices French bread

Heat the oil in a frying-pan and add the slices of black pudding or spicy sausage. Cover and cook for 1 minute on each side. Toast the bread and place a piece of black pudding or spicy sausage on top. Serve immediately.

MADRID SNAILS
IN A SPICY SAUCE
Caracoles Madrileños en Salsa Picante

Despite the fact that various Spanish food historians insist on telling me that it is in Aragón and Valencia that snails are truly appreciated, I have also often eaten them in Andalusia where the small ones are known as *cabrillas* and the large ones as *caracoles*. All are sold in plastic nets, and the price of the bag of snails includes the aromatic herbs to cook them with, which combine with a selection of spices, sold in little packets especially for this delicacy. Snails can be insipid, so they tend to be cooked in spicy sauces, or as part of a substantial soup.

I most frequently eat snails in the taverns of Madrid in the spring. The best are vine snails which feed on the first vine leaves, just as they do in autumn when they can damage the grape harvest.

SERVES 4

1 kg (2 lb) cleaned snails in their shells
100 ml (3½ fl oz) olive oil
1 small Spanish onion, peeled and chopped
1 green pepper, de-seeded and chopped
1 red pepper, de-seeded and chopped

1 garlic clove, peeled and chopped
1 red chilli pepper, de-seeded and chopped
1 sprig of thyme, chopped
½ teaspoon paprika
Salt and freshly ground black pepper
3 tablespoons water

Put the snails in a large pan and cover with plenty of salted water. Bring to the boil, drain and refill the pan with water. Bring to the boil again.

Meanwhile, heat the oil in a frying-pan, and fry the onions, peppers and garlic for about 5 minutes until soft. When they are almost cooked, add the chilli pepper, thyme and paprika and season to taste with salt and freshly ground black pepper. Simmer for 5 minutes, adding cold water if necessary. Drain the snails and transfer them to a flameproof casserole. Pour the sauce over them, cover and simmer gently for 1 hour.

QUAILS with HERB DRESSING
Codornices con Mojo

The quail is the smallest of the hen family. It is more delicate than partridge, especially in the autumn before the migration season begins. They are mostly battery-bred now and can easily be bought in packs from the supermarket. They are not as tasty but are still very appetizing if cooked well.

SERVES 4

6 slices of bacon
6 quail
1 Spanish onion, peeled and minced
6 tablespoons olive oil
1 teaspoon chopped fresh thyme
1 glass dry white wine
Salt
400 g (14 oz) potatoes, peeled and diced

For the dressing

3 tablespoons olive oil
1 tablespoon white wine vinegar
1 sprig of mint, finely chopped
1 small sprig of thyme, finely chopped

Lightly fry the bacon, then wrap 1 slice around each quail. Place the birds in a flameproof casserole dish. Add the onion, half the oil and the thyme and cook for a few minutes until just brown on all sides. Add the wine, bring to the boil, cover and simmer over a medium heat for 45 minutes until tender.

Meanwhile, heat the remaining oil and fry the potatoes with the salt until golden-brown and crisp. Mix together the dressing ingredients. Add the potatoes to the quails and serve with the dressing.

SOUPS AND STEWS
Sopas y Potajes

The Spaniard is a soup-eater both by tradition and by inclination. Country cooking all over Spain has produced many soups which are an integral part of people's diet, whether as a first course at lunch, in the winter, or at dinner on many days of the year.

I will always remember my Basque grandmother, Julia, arriving at our house one fine day with a heavy-lidded cast-iron pot called an *olla*. Inside was a *caldo*, a broth, that she promised would make us grow if we drank it. Into the pot she would put a boiling hen in some water and, tied lightly with muslin, a few cloves and sprigs of parsley, some saffron and cinnamon, and half a bay leaf.

The *olla* is one of the traditional cooking pots which come in many shapes and sizes and are all part of the catalogue of utensils that Spanish cooking has employed for many generations to prepare hot and cold soups and stews. *Pucheros* are made of glazed earthenware, painted metal and enamel, or aluminium. Andalusian *lebrillos* are the earthenware bowls used for mixing ingredients, and *dornillos* are the wooden mixing bowls. Most common of all is the earthenware *cazuela*, the flameproof casserole dish used for all kinds of dishes in Spanish cooking.

The marvellous tradition of the Spanish *caldos* is alive and well in many villages in the countryside around Córdoba, where visitors are regaled on cold mornings with a light broth or *caldito*, known locally as travellers' stock. It can be found in Navarra, too, where they still call it invalid broth because this substantial, fairly strongly flavoured stock was originally fed, in rural Spain, to the sick and to recently delivered mothers.

The secret of the *caldo* is to cook it on the very lowest heat for two to three hours, which gives the most exquisite, complex flavour. Sometimes they may turn out a little greasy, but all you need to do is to put the casserole in the fridge for a while for the fat to solidify on the surface so that it is easy to remove.

The *caldos* from the *cocidos*, which are cooked under many names all over the Peninsula, are traditionally served with thin pasta or rice. Bread and garlic soup, those made with minced egg, rice and ham, the almond and monkfish soups of Moorish origin and the complicated but richly flavoured fish soups represent the variety of the tradition throughout the regions of Spain. The Basques delight in the simplicity of their *porrusalda* of potato and leek, the Madrileños in their fish and rice soup known as *sopa al cuarto de hora* – the quarter of an hour soup – and the people of the Levantine city of Morella are devoted to the profiteroles they float in their wonderful *caldo*. Each locality has a special broth to settle the stomach or soothe the quick temper.

There is also a multitude of cold soups, some light, some creamy, but all most welcome on those summer days when the heat is oppressive and the body says no to food. In Andalusia, the *gazpacho* season is hailed by the arrival of the fine weather. It is amusing to see how everybody, even the foreigners living there, talk about whether or not the tomatoes are yet right, for it is vital that they are just so if this deliciously refreshing cold soup is to be at its most richly flavoursome.

In the Castilian tongue, the word *potaje* does not mean the same as the French *potage*, which embraces only certain kinds of soup. For us this word has retained its primitive meaning of a stock with meat, vegetables and pulses – solid ingredients – that has been cooked in a *puchero* or *olla*.

Vegetable stews and other dishes, the ones I call 'substantial', deserve a separate entry on the grounds of their originality and quality within Spain's culinary repertoire. The recipes are based on the Roman chick pea and the ancient lentil – which we always use from the last crop – and beans of all kinds: white, pinto, almost black, with or without eyes. These are most frequently cooked with pig meats of one kind or another. Pork gives them great flavour, especially belly pork, *chorizo* sausages, *morcillas* or black pudding, *butifarra* or white pudding and, king of them all, Serrano ham. Also in this group come the Lenten *potajes* made with vegetables, pulses and often salt cod.

These are dishes cooked in the *cortijos*, hamlets, villages, town and schools of the old Roman Hispania, but in the cities, where the role of women has changed and modestly priced restaurants are disappearing daily, *potaje* is served less frequently. They always have been part of home cooking where the best food in Spain is still eaten. It is also wonderful to see a few of these regional specialities are now cooked to perfection by chefs at some of Spain's most sophisticated restaurants. These serious cooks are the inheritors and guardians of recipes which have for the most part been passed on orally.

If you should ever find yourself in the Basque city of Tolosa in November, ask for directions to the Beotibar *frontón* court. A competition is held there once a year that has nothing to do with the ball game. It is a cooking competition to celebrate the small, almost black, beans this area produces in the vegetable garden of the *caserío*, the Basque country farmhouse. The rules are fairly basic: each competitor is given one kilogram of beans to which can be added whatever ingredients they like as long as the bean predominates. The beans must be cooked in the *frontón* court between nine o'clock in the morning and one in the afternoon, at which time the dishes are submitted for judgement. Ask the winner to let you taste their creation and you will understand why beans are one of my favourite weaknesses.

I would recommend Fino sherry or Manzanilla, Albariño or white oak-aged Rioja with some of the soups and broths, while full-bodied reds like Ribera del Duero or Toro might be perfect with a serious bean stew from Asturias or Alava.

Mussel soup
Sopa de Mejillones

I can still recall a wonderful boat trip to the rafts in the Ría of Villagarcía de Arosa in Pontevedra, where mussels, oysters and scallops grow in abundance. The mussels we used to make this soup were small but deliciously full of flavour. Although the dash of *eau-de-vie* that is made in Galicia removes the soup from its original fishing village origins, it does give a wonderful touch of sophistication.

SERVES 6

60 mussels, scrubbed and
   beards removed
120 ml (4 fl oz) olive oil
1 Spanish onion, peeled and
   finely chopped
5 ripe tomatoes, skinned,
   de-seeded and finely
   chopped
1.5 litres (2½ pints) water

3 slices bread, crusts
   removed
5 garlic cloves, peeled
1 small sprig of parsley
1 small cinnamon stick
1 small glass aguardiente,
   eau-de-vie or brandy
Salt and freshly ground
   black pepper

Place the mussels in a large pan and cover with cold water.
Bring to the boil and boil for a few minutes just until the
mussels open. Do not overcook the mussels. Strain and
reserve the cooking liquor. Shell the mussels, discarding any
which remain closed, and put them to one side.

Heat the oil in a large pan on a very high heat and fry the
onion until it softens, then add the tomatoes and fry until you
have a good *sofrito*. Moisten it with a little of the mussel
cooking liquor and add enough water to make up to 2.5 litres
(4½ pints). Bring the soup to the boil.

Meanwhile, toast the bread and dice it. Use a mortar and
pestle to pound the garlic, parsley and cinnamon, mix in the
aguardiente, eau-de-vie or brandy and add the mixture to
the soup with the bread as the soup begins to boil. Simmer for
a few minutes, then add the mussels and blend all the ingredients together with a whisk or hand blender until creamy.
Rub through a sieve if necessary. Do not allow the soup to
thicken too much; add a little more water if necessary. Season
to taste with salt and freshly ground black pepper and serve.

FISH SOUP
Sopa de Pescado

This is a substantial, wonderfully strongly flavoured soup which I would recommend for lunch-time. It shows off to perfection the traditional Spanish method of thickening soup with pieces of bread. This is one of those dishes that is much better made the day before it is needed then re-heated gently.

SERVES 4

2 leeks
2 medium Spanish onions, peeled
500 g (1 lb 2 oz) monkfish, cleaned
2 litres (3½ pints) water
100 ml (3½ fl oz) olive oil
1 glass Spanish brandy
1 stick French bread, crusts removed and diced

2 garlic cloves, peeled and chopped
200 g (7 oz) uncooked prawns, peeled
500 g (1 lb 2 oz) tomatoes, skinned, de-seeded and chopped
200 g (7 oz) clams, scrubbed

Cut 1 leek and 1 onion into chunks and place in a large saucepan with the fish and water. Bring to the boil, cover and simmer for 30 minutes to make a stock. Strain the fish and vegetables and reserve the stock. Remove and discard the skin and bones from the fish and cut the fish into pieces.

Finely chop the remaining onion. Heat 4 tablespoons of oil in a large flameproof casserole, add the onion and fry until well browned, then add the brandy. Add the bread and sauté, using a wooden spoon to turn it in the oil. Pour in the fish stock, making sure that the bread is covered. Reduce to a low heat, cover and simmer for 1 hour, adding more stock if the mixture looks too thick.

Chop the remaining leek. Heat the rest of the oil in a frying-pan and sauté the garlic, leek and vegetables from the stock until lightly browned, then add the tomatoes and cook until soft. Purée the mixture, then gradually add it to the bread mixture, mixing well, and simmer for 5 minutes. Add the fish, prawns and clams. Simmer gently until and clams open, discarding any that remain closed. Remove from the heat and serve.

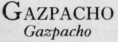

GAZPACHO
Gazpacho

There are as many *gazpacho* recipes as there are people who make it. Manuela, a housewife from Aracena, has used her father's recipe for the last 40 years. Every day, she used to take the great earthenware pot out to the 12 hot and tired workers tending her land who eagerly awaited the arrival of the refreshing soup and home-made bread. The pepper Manuela uses is one of the long, thin, fine-fleshed varieties, but the more rounded peppers available in Britain make an equally tasty soup. Most more commercial *gazpachos* are garnished with tomato, pepper, bread and cucumber, although only cucumber is added in Aracena.

SERVES 6–8

*1.25 kg (2½ lb) ripe
tomatoes, skinned and
de-seeded*
*1 cucumber, peeled and
roughly chopped*
*2 green peppers, de-seeded
and roughly chopped*
*½ Spanish onion, peeled
and roughly chopped*

*2 tablespoons white wine
vinegar*
250 ml (8 fl oz) olive oil
*120 g (4½ oz) fresh
breadcrumbs*
Salt
*1 slice yesterday's bread,
diced*
Cold water
Ice cubes

Reserve 1 tomato, a small piece of cucumber and a small piece of pepper for garnish. Place the remaining tomatoes, cucumber and pepper with the onion, vinegar, oil and bread-crumbs, in batches if necessary, in a food processor and blend to a fine consistency. The tomatoes should yield enough juice, but if necessary add a little water. Season to taste with salt. When all the ingredients are well blended, transfer to a soup tureen or serving dish and refrigerate.

Dice the reserved tomato, cucumber and pepper and place them and the bread in separate bowls to be used as a garnish. When ready to serve, add enough cold water to the soup to achieve the consistency you prefer. Stir in a few ice cubes so that the soup is well chilled.

GALICIAN BROTH
Caldo Gallego

Caldo, Galician broth, is a dish that is served in all Galician restaurants and is cooked on a daily basis. One day in autumn whilst shopping in Santiago market I asked one of the owners of a bean and chick pea stall if she knew of a recipe for Galician broth. After exchanging various ideas with the nearby stall owners she gave me the following recipe.

SERVES 6

300 g (11 oz) haricot beans
2 small veal or beef bones
300 g (11 oz) gammon
2 litres (3½ pints) water
25 g (1 oz) lard

500 g (1 lb 2 oz) potatoes,
  peeled and diced
450 g (1 lb) spinach or
  turnip tops
Salt
A little paprika

Soak the haricot beans overnight in cold water then drain and rinse.

Place the beans, bones, gammon and water in a large flameproof earthenware casserole and bring to the boil. Add the lard, bring back to the boil, cover and boil very gently for 1½ hours. Add the potatoes and boil for a further 6 minutes. Add the spinach or turnip tops and boil for a further 4 or 5 minutes until all the vegetables are cooked. Remove the bones and season to taste with salt and a little paprika. If the broth is not as thick as you like it, take out a spoonful of potatoes and beans, mash them finely and stir them back into the broth. Serve hot.

WHITE BEANS WITH CLAMS
Judías Blancas con Almejas

La Granja butter beans are renowned and, together with the ones produced in El Barco in the north-west, are the best in Spain. They are ideal for this dish but any large white butter beans can be used. Here they combine beautifully with clams, my favourite shellfish.

SERVES 4

600 g (1 lb 5 oz) large white butter beans
½ Spanish onion, peeled and chopped
1 garlic clove, peeled and crushed
1 sprig of parsley, chopped
½ bay leaf
1 tablespoon olive oil
300 g (11 oz) clams, scrubbed
2 strands saffron
1 tablespoon fresh breadcrumbs
Salt

Soak the beans overnight in cold water, then drain and rinse.

Place the beans in a flameproof casserole, then add the onion, garlic, parsley, bay leaf and oil. Shake the casserole to mix the ingredients, then cover them with cold water, put on the lid and bring to the boil. Leave a slight gap between the lid and the rim of the casserole and simmer for about 1 hour until the beans are cooked. Add extra cold water as necessary to make sure the beans remain covered so that the skins do not come off.

Meanwhile place the clams in another saucepan with a little cold water. Place over a moderate heat and transfer to another dish as they open. Discard any that remain closed. Use a sharp knife to cut through the hinge between the shells and remove the clams from the shells, or leave them in the shell if you prefer. Strain the cooking liquid through a fine cloth and allow it to cool completely. Lightly roast the saffron for a few seconds in a dry pan over a moderate heat then crush it and add it to a little of the cooled liquor. When the beans are nearly ready, add the clams, the cooled liquid, the saffron and the breadcrumbs. Shake to make sure the ingredients are well mixed, and cook gently for 15 minutes. Season with salt. Once the beans are ready, remove from the heat, discard the bay leaf and allow to rest for a few minutes before serving.

BEAN STEW FROM ASTURIAS
Fabada Asturiana

The principality of Asturias, in the north of Spain, is bathed by the Cantabrian sea. It has given Spanish cookery a dish of which we all feel rather proud: this lovely substantial stew richly flavoured with spicy sausages. I confess it was not always such a favourite with me: as a child I can remember crying bitter tears on Tuesdays which were *fabada* days at school!

SERVES 4

*1 kg (2 lb) large white
    butter beans*
500 g (1 lb 2 oz) gammon
*250 g (9 oz) black pudding
    sausage*
*250 g (9 oz) good quality
    chorizo sausages*

*100 g (4 oz) belly pork,
    rinded*
2 tablespoons olive oil
2–3 strands saffron
Salt

Soak the beans overnight in cold water, then drain and rinse.

Place the beans, gammon, black pudding, *chorizos*, belly pork and olive oil (which will improve the texture of the beans) in a large flameproof casserole, cover with cold water and bring to the boil. Skim carefully, then reduce the heat to a simmer, leave the lid slightly off, and simmer for about 1 hour. Top up with extra cold water as necessary to make sure the beans remain covered so that the skins do not come off. Keep an eye on the casserole to make sure the water is only simmering and give it an occasional shake to prevent the beans sticking to the bottom.

Lightly roast the saffron for a few seconds in a dry pan over a moderate heat then crush it. Half-way through cooking, add the saffron to the pan. When the beans are cooked, check and season to taste with salt, but bear in mind that the gammon and sausages will give out some salt.

If you want a thicker broth, remove some of the beans, press them through a sieve and stir them back into the stew.

Cut the meat into pieces and allow the stew to rest for 20 minutes before serving the *fabada* in the casserole or a warmed serving dish.

Ⓥ CASTILIAN GARLIC SOUP
Sopa de Ajo Castellana

This recipe makes a soup that is lighter than that normally served in the restaurants of Castile, where they usually fry the garlic and paprika in olive oil and mix this into the boiling water with the salt and oregano. The garlic taste in this soup is deliciously subtle and the pieces of bread should be cut quite small so that they do not swell too much and become 'soupy' and too strongly flavoured with paprika.

SERVES 4

1.5 litres (2½ pints) water
3 teaspoons salt
4 garlic cloves, peeled
1 tablespoon olive oil
1½ teaspoons paprika,
   sweet or hot

25 g (1 oz) bread, crusts
   removed and diced
1 egg, beaten (optional)
A pinch of chopped fresh
   oregano

Heat the water and salt in a deep flameproof casserole. Use a mortar and pestle to pound the garlic with the oil and paprika to taste. Blend well, then add to the stock and bring to the boil. Add the bread and egg, if using. Check and adjust the seasoning if necessary and add the oregano. Remove from the heat immediately, cover and leave for 10 minutes before serving.

This soup can be served in individual earthenware dishes, in which case the egg is added after the soup has been poured. Cover the dishes and allow the soup to rest before eating.

POTATOES WITH CLAMS IN THE GRAND MANNER
Patatas con Almejas a la Importancia

My mother used to cook potatoes in this way but without the clams. This particular recipe was given to me by Tomás Herranz, chef at the famous Madrid restaurant El Cenador del Prado. His dish is a far cry from my mother's, but both are equally delicious Basque-style recipes with a smooth sauce and a green flash given by the parsley.

SERVES 4

1 kg (2 lb) potatoes, peeled and sliced

4 tablespoons plain flour

3 eggs, beaten

1 garlic clove, peeled and crushed

2 teaspoons chopped fresh parsley

Salt

100 ml (3½ fl oz) olive oil

For the sauce

4 tablespoons olive oil

100 g (4 oz) Spanish onions, peeled and finely chopped

1 garlic clove, peeled and crushed

1 tablespoon plain flour

1 tablespoon chopped fresh parsley

500 ml (17 fl oz) vegetable stock

20 clams, scrubbed

Coat the potato slices in flour. Beat the eggs with the garlic, parsley and a little salt. Heat the oil, dip the potato slices in the egg and fry them until light golden and cooked through. Drain on kitchen paper.

To make the sauce, heat the oil and fry the onion gently until soft, then add the garlic and fry for 1 minute. Stir in the flour and parsley and cook for 1 minute, then add the vegetable stock, bring to the boil and simmer for 5 minutes. Taste and season with salt if necessary. Pour the sauce into a flameproof earthenware dish, add the potatoes and clams and cook for about 10 minutes until the clams open up, shaking the pan occasionally. Discard any clams that remain closed. Serve immediately.

WINTER BROTH WITH PROFITEROLES
Caldo con Profiteroles

This *caldo* or broth is made in the historic city of Morella in Castellón, which stand 1500 metres above sea level. During the harsh winters, the city is often cut off by snow, providing the perfect opportunity to try this particular dish. Instead of the pasta generally used in the *caldos* in these parts – vermicelli, tiny star shapes and so on – this one uses little puffs of choux pastry. The original recipe makes the profiteroles just from water, oil, flour and salt, but I have adapted it to the way I make them at home. My profiteroles are filled with an unusual stuffing of chicken livers and pine kernels and dance on the top of the beautiful clear broth.

SERVES 6

For the broth

1 medium-sized corn-fed chicken	1 Spanish onion, peeled and quartered
1 Serrano ham or dry-cured ham bone	1 turnip, cut into chunks
225 g (8 oz) oxtail	1 carrot, cut into chunks
1 leek, cut into chunks	100 g (4 oz) chick peas

For the profiteroles

250 ml (8 fl oz) water	100 g (4 oz) plain flour
2 tablespoons olive oil	2 eggs, beaten
Salt and freshly ground black pepper	

For the filling

250 g (9 oz) chicken livers	100 g (4 oz) pine kernels
1 egg yolk	

Soak the chick peas overnight in cold water, then drain and rinse.

To make the broth, place all the broth ingredients in a large pan and cover with cold water. Bring to the boil, then cover and simmer over a low heat for at least 3 hours. Strain once.

To make the profiteroles, pre-heat the oven to 180°C/350°F/Gas 4. Place the water, oil, salt and freshly ground black pepper in a saucepan and bring to the boil. Remove the pan from the heat and pour in the flour. Mix well until the mixture forms a ball which comes away cleanly from the sides of the pan. Transfer the pastry to a glass bowl and gradually add the eggs, a little at a time. Spoon the mixture into a piping bag and pipe small balls, about the size of a small walnut, on to a greased baking sheet. Bake in the oven for 15 minutes until well risen and golden-brown. Cut a slit in the base of the profiteroles and leave to cool slightly.

Meanwhile, place the chicken livers, eggs yolk and pine kernels in a food processor and blend until the mixture is creamy. Pipe the filling into the profiteroles and drop them into the soup. Simmer for 2 minutes to heat through. The filling will cook in the hot soup. Serve immediately.

LENTILS WITH CHORIZO AND PORK
Lentejas con Chorizo

Now that, outside Spain, we can buy genuine *chorizo* from beyond the Pyrenees, instead of the strange preserved meats purveyed until recently under false names, I recommend that you try this way of serving *chorizo* with lentils. This is one of the pulses on which my generation was raised. Because of their nutritional value and delicious taste, I feel lentils should be used more in schools as well as in the home, not merely as an ingredient in the cuisine created by avant-garde cooks, but as a part of the traditional cooking of many countries.

SERVES 4

500 g (1 lb 2 oz) small
    brown lentils
2 leeks or Spanish onions,
    peeled and chopped
2 carrots, chopped
2 garlic cloves, peeled and
    halved
100 g (4 oz) chorizo *sausage*

100 g (4 oz) belly pork,
    rinded
1 bay leaf
3 tablespoons olive oil
½ teaspoon salt
1 Spanish onion, peeled and
    finely chopped

Soak the lentils for a few hours in cold water, then drain and rinse.

Place them in a large pan or flameproof earthenware casserole and just cover with cold water. Add the leeks or onions, carrots, garlic, *chorizo*, pork, bay leaf, half the oil and the salt. Bring to the boil, cover and simmer gently for about 30 minutes until the lentils begin to swell and soften and the meat is cooked. For best results, allow the lentils to cook slowly.

Meanwhile, heat the remaining oil and fry the onion until soft to make a *sofrito*. Stir this into the lentils, remove the bay leaf and cut the pork and *chorizo* into pieces. Return them to the pan to heat through before serving.

TOLOSA BEAN STEW
Judías de Tolosa

This is dish from my beloved Basque Country. It is a classic of the hamlets where black beans are harvested twice a year. The main feature of this dish is that the broth becomes very thick. This takes many hours of slow cooking – no short cuts!

Do remember that dark beans must be boiled during the cooking process to destroy the toxins they contain.

SERVES 4–6

500 g (1 lb 2 oz) black
  beans
1 small Spanish onion,
  peeled and halved
Salt
100 ml (3½ fl oz) olive oil
120 g (4½ oz) belly pork or
  salt pork, rinded
120 g (4½ oz) chorizo
  sausage

120 g (4½ oz) black
  pudding sausage with
  onion
1 large green pepper,
  de-seeded and finely
  chopped
1 garlic clove, peeled and
  finely chopped

Soak the beans overnight in cold water, then drain and rinse.

Place the beans and half the onion in a deep flameproof earthenware casserole, cover with cold water to 2.5 cm (1 in) above the beans and season with salt. Bring to the boil and boil rapidly for 15 minutes, then cover and leave over a very low heat for about 4 hours. As the beans absorb the water, add a little cold salted water, a little at a time. Just before the beans are ready, by which time the stock will have thickened, shake the pan gently to thicken the broth further.

While the beans are simmering, heat a little oil and fry the pork, chorizo and black pudding for a few minutes. Test the pudding as you cook so that you do not overcook it. Cut each of the meats into 4.

Finely chop the remaining onion. Heat the remaining oil and fry the onion, pepper and garlic to make a refrito. Add the refrito and meats to the cooked beans. Check and adjust the seasoning if necessary. Bring gently to the boil and simmer for 10 minutes before serving.

HAM AND EGG SOUP
Sopa de Picadillo

This soup is originally from Andalusia and is one to revive you. The stock is almost opaque, highlighting the lovely combination of colours of the egg and ham which make up the *picadillo*. The soup is traditionally served with a sprig of Moorish mint.

SERVES 4

For the stock

250 g (9 oz) chick peas
3 litres (5¼ pints) water
2 large Serrano ham or dry-cured ham bones (optional)
1 kg (2 lb) veal or beef bones, blanched
3 carrots, cut into large pieces

2 sticks celery, cut into large pieces
3 leeks, cut into large pieces
½ boiling chicken
300 g (11 oz) potatoes, peeled
1 teaspoon salt

150 g (5 oz) long-grain rice
100 g (4 oz) ham, diced

2 hard-boiled eggs, chopped
1 sprig of mint, chopped

Soak the chick peas overnight in cold water, then drain and rinse.

Place all the stock ingredients in a large pan and bring to the boil. Cover and simmer gently for 2½–3 hours to make a good stock. Remove the chicken, bone it, cut the meat into pieces and keep it warm. Strain the stock ready to use for the broth.

Place the stock, rice and ham in a large pan, bring to the

boil and simmer for 15 minutes or until the rice is cooked. Transfer to a warned serving dish and add the chicken, eggs and mint.

YOU HAVE BEEN WARNED!

Ⓥ COLD ALMOND SOUP FROM MÁLAGA
Ajo Blanco de Málaga

The cold garlic and almond soups which are so well made in Málaga and Córdoba have come down to us from the Middle Ages, when the Moors were busy enriching Al-Andalus. This recipe is one that José Antonio Valdespino makes in his restaurant La Mesa Redonda in Jerez and in my view it is masterly. José Antonio's family use their own sherry vinegar: its concentration and colour are unrivalled and it complements the garlic and almonds to perfection. The soup is easy to make, full of flavour, and has the most wonderful rich, smooth texture – perfect for a summer meal or a light entrée to a sophisticated dinner.

SERVES 4

75 g (3 oz) almonds,
   blanched and skinned
3 garlic cloves, peeled
Salt
900 ml (1½ pints) water
100 g (4 oz) fresh
   breadcrumbs, soaked in
   water

6 tablespoons olive oil
1½ tablespoons sherry
   vinegar
Ice cubes
120 g (4½ oz) white or
   black grapes

Use a mortar and pestle to pound the almonds and garlic with a pinch of salt, adding a few tablespoons of water until you have a fine paste. (You can use a food processor to do this but the texture will be different.) Add the breadcrumbs, beating continuously. Gradually beat in the oil a drop at a time, as for a mayonnaise. Add the sherry vinegar, and thin the soup by adding the remaining water and a pinch of salt. Serve with a few ice cubes in the bowls and garnish with the grapes.

CHICK PEAS WITH SPINACH AND SALT COD
Potaje de Garbanzos, Espinacas y Bacalao

Stews are a favourite during Lent, when cooks are obliged to resort to all their ingenuity to make up for the foods they are not allowed to serve. I still recall a memorable lunch in the fortress of Carmona. The menu began with a *revuelto* of fine green asparagus, followed by a stew of baby spinach, chick peas and a dash of salt cod, with a walnut sponge for dessert served with fresh apricot and bitter orange conserve.

SOUPS AND STEWS

SERVES 4

200 g (7 oz) dried salt cod
300 g (11 oz) chick peas
2 Spanish onions, peeled
2 litres (3½ pints) water
1 teaspoon salt

1 carrot, chopped
½ bay leaf
400 g (14 oz) spinach, stalks
   removed
100 ml (3½ fl oz) olive oil

Soak the cod in water for 24–36 hours, depending on the thickness of the pieces, changing the water at least 3 times. Drain and flake the fish. Soak the chick peas overnight in cold water, then drain and rinse.

Slice 1 onion. Place the water, salt, sliced onion, carrot and bay leaf in a large pan and bring to the boil. As soon as the water begins to bubble, add the chick peas. Bring back to the boil, cover and simmer gently for 2–3 hours until the chick peas are cooked, adding a little extra water if necessary.

Meanwhile, cook the spinach in a very little salted water for 3 minutes, then drain and chop. Chop the remaining onion. Heat the oil and fry the onion until golden, then add the cod and cook, stirring continuously, for 1–2 minutes.

When the chick peas are cooked, remove the bay leaf, add the cod and onion mixture and the spinach, boil for 2 minutes. If you like a thicker stew, you can purée some of the chick peas then return them to the stew before serving.

CHICK PEA BROTH WITH MONKFISH AND CLAMS
Potaje de Garbanzos con Rape y Almejas

There is a little mountain village called Ezcarai in the Rioja Alavesa, not far from the ski resort that has taken the same name. This stew is made at the Echaurren Hotel by Marisa the owner, and it is very much her personal recipe for Lent. The strong combination of flavours complement one another beautifully. It takes a little longer to prepare than some of the other recipes, but is well worth the trouble.

SERVES 4

250 g (9 oz) chick peas
1 teaspoon salt
A pinch of bicarbonate of soda
1 leek, cut into chunks
5 garlic cloves
2 Spanish onions, peeled
2 tablespoons olive oil
450 g (1 lb) monkfish, cut into chunks
4 tomatoes, skinned, de-seeded and chopped
250 g (9 oz) clams, scrubbed
1 sprig of parsley
1 red pepper, skinned, de-seeded and chopped
1 green pepper, skinned, de-seeded and chopped
350 g (12 oz) long-grain rice
100 g (4 oz) chard or spinach, chopped
2 hard-boiled eggs, roughly chopped
Salt

Soak the chick peas overnight in cold water with the salt and bicarbonate of soda. If the chick peas are old or the water hard, add a little more bicarbonate of soda.

Rinse the chick peas thoroughly in running water. Place them in a large saucepan and add the leek, 2 whole unpeeled cloves of garlic and 1 whole peeled onion. Cover with fresh water, bring to the boil and simmer for 2 hours until the chick peas are almost cooked. Add a little fresh cold water during the cooking process, if necessary; never add boiling water. It is important to stir the peas only with a wooden spoon, and very carefully, or just shake the pan.

Meanwhile, heat 1 tablespoon of oil and chop the remaining onion. Fry the onion and monkfish lightly on all sides to seal. Heat 1 tablespoon of oil in another pan and lightly fry the tomatoes. Add them to the fish, then put to one side.

Place the clams in a saucepan with a little cold water. Place over a moderate head and transfer to another dish as they open. Discard any that remain closed. Use a mortar and pestle to pound 1 peeled clove of garlic with the parsley or finely chop them together with a knife. Peel and chop the remaining garlic. Heat the oil and fry the chopped garlic for 2 minutes, then add the peppers and fry for a further 3 minutes.

Stir the rice into the chick peas and simmer for 10 minutes. Add the chard or spinach and continue to simmer until the chick peas are cooked. Add the garlic and parsley, and monkfish and the clams, followed by the garlic and peppers and the hard-boiled eggs. Season to taste with salt. Cover and simmer the broth gently until ready to serve, without allowing it to become too thick.

Ⓥ # GYPSIES' HOTPOT
Olla Gitana

I have always wondered why this dish is named after the gypsies, but so far no one has been able to give me a satisfactory answer. It could be because of its lovely colouring and its contrasting sweet and sour flavour.

SERVES 4

250 g (9 oz) chick peas
2.5 litres (4½ pints) water
250 g (9 oz) green beans, sliced diagonally into 3 cm (1¼ in) lengths
150 g (5 oz) pumpkin, peeled and diced into 4 cm (1½ in) cubes
3 pears, peeled, cored and diced
Salt and freshly ground black pepper
100 ml (3½ fl oz) olive oil
1 Spanish onion, peeled and finely chopped

1 teaspoon paprika
2 ripe tomatoes, skinned, de-seeded and chopped
1 small slice bread, crusts removed and diced
1 garlic clove, peeled and chopped
10 almonds, toasted and skinned
2–3 strands saffron
2 tablespoons hot vegetable stock
2 tablespoons white wine vinegar

Soak the chick peas overnight in cold water, drain and rinse.

Bring the water to the boil in a large pan, add the chick peas, cover and simmer gently for 1 hour. Gradually add the green beans, pumpkin and pears without letting the soup go off the boil. Season with salt and freshly ground black pepper. Continue to simmer gently for a further 1–2 hours until everything is tender.

Heat half the oil and fry the onion until golden, then add the paprika followed by the tomatoes and fry gently until the tomatoes are cooked. Meanwhile, heat the remaining oil and fry the bread and garlic until browned. Use a mortar and pestle to pound the bread, garlic and almonds to a fine paste. Crush the saffron then dissolve it in the stock, mix in the vinegar and dissolve the bread and garlic paste in the liquid.

When the chick peas are almost cooked, stir the onion and tomato mixture and the bread and garlic mixture into the beans and heat through. Adjust the seasoning if necessary and serve very hot from a warmed soup tureen.

VEGETABLES
Verduras

In terms of production and market availability, Spain has access to an excellent and sophisticated garden in which the majority of vegetable varieties are grown all year round. There is a general tendency, though, to overcook them. It is also true to say that in some culinary traditions, for example in most of the Basque Country, vegetables were not fully appreciated until a few years ago when the professionals began to create new trends.

In general vegetables and salads have always been served at least once a day, not merely as another ingredient, but as a course by themselves. All shared the role of being the first course in the week's diet. Look at a Spanish restaurant menu: after the soups, you will see a section of vegetable dishes.

I can still see my husband Philip's face when, as a newly-wed, I made him cauliflower cheese. I served it as I had been taught, as a first course accompanied by red wine. Later, I produced another plate for the meat. The expression on his face was a complete mystery to me until I sat down to my first formal English dinner and was served meat, gravy, unseasoned and unadorned vegetables, carrots and peas, and plain boiled potatoes on the same plate. I scanned the centre of the table for olive oil and vinegar, but found only salt, pepper and a few one-portion packs of butter with which my companions had already begun to anoint their vegetables. This was so different to my own Spanish traditions.

Vegetable dishes such as *menestra* and *pisto* illustrate the Spanish use of vegetables at its best. *Menestra*, a traditional dish from the Navarrese and Riojan schools of cooking, shows off the wealth of produce grown in the valleys of the Ebro river and its tributaries. The main ingredients are usually small, tender artichokes, the white part of the chard cut into small pieces, freshly shelled peas, new-born green beans, asparagus and, depending on the cook's personal taste, a little spicy *chorizo*, ham and perhaps a hard-boiled egg added towards the end. The secret is to know the specific cooking times the various ingredients require, as they are all cooked separately in the first instance, then combined together.

The last time I had a *pisto* of the *Manchego* variety, as this particular one is called, was quite recently in the dining-room of a beautiful house on a Taray lagoon. The affable, friendly and plump cook had spent a good part of the morning cutting up the ingredients: courgettes, green peppers, onions and potatoes, which she cooked all together in a large saucepan. A few minutes before serving the *pisto*, having already set a mould of boiled rice on the platter, she added some beaten eggs that she allowed just to set. I enjoyed it so much that for dinner I asked her to give me a little of the *pisto* that had been left over at lunch-time. Cold, it was even more delicious.

Onion, tomato and red and green peppers are essential to our cooking, and the majority of our dishes would not exist without them. This is especially true of onion, and we know how to extract the best of its flavours by cooking it for just the right length of time and in just the right way.

Since living away from Spain, the vegetables I have missed most over the years are artichokes, chard, and thin, green asparagus. Both fresh and tinned artichokes are always present on the majority of Spanish restaurant menus in one guise or another. I prefer them small, simply boiled in plenty of water with a few drops of lemon to keep the colour green, drained and tossed with a little onion and olive oil. I enjoy chard and spinach cooked in the same way, substituting the onion with some unpeeled garlic. In Valencia, the smallest, tiniest artichokes are sliced and grilled, as are the small, tender and yet firm new season's green asparagus, which I love to eat with just a touch of sea salt. These asparagus are also delicious in an egg and prawn *revuelto*, something like a scrambled egg dish, as are the many varieties of mushroom and other fungi that are gathered across the Peninsula.

Wild mushrooms are also an important part of the Spanish repertoire, although recipes for them come from specific areas. The Basques and Catalans have an incomparable fascination with them, and people there are prepared to pay anything for certain varieties. You need a visit to the local markets – small village ones or large ones like the Boquería in the Ramblas of Barcelona – to appreciate the adulation lavished on them.

In springtime, the *zizak*, as this mushroom is called in Basque, is much sought after. One of the *Tricholoma* family, it has a delicate and sumptuous taste. Then there are the *Morchela esculenta*, also known as *Karraspina*, which are grilled with a garlic and parsley stuffing. In summer, *Russulas* make their appearance in the markets. My brother loves them, especially the ones called *Guibelurdinas*, the *Russula cynaxanta* and *cirecens*, which are served raw, marinated in olive oil and cider vinegar.

August is the month of the deep orange-coloured *Amanita caesarea*. Although its name is similar to that of one of the dangerous ones, the *caesarea* is a real treat just quickly tossed in half butter and half olive oil.

Autumn is the best season for hunting fungi, and brings

the delicious *Boletus*, which is best sautéd with fresh herbs and a hint of garlic. Then, in November and December, we have a great abundance of *Lactarious delicious*, called *Níscalos* in Castilian, *Rovellons* in Catalan, and *Esnegorri* in the Basque Country. These are the only ones I cook with wine – a little white wine, that is. It is not always easy to cook mushrooms well, and there is a proverb in Navarra which says that the secret is to know them all and to know exactly how long to cook each one. I would add that this is, in fact, the secret of all Spanish vegetable cookery.

We know that the Incas cooked peppers, or capsicums, and that they were brought to Spain by the conquistadores in the sixteenth century. Ever since then, peppers – which are as tasty as they are colourful – have been closely linked to all Spain's cooking styles. Whether served as a first course or as a main dish, they are the latest in fashionable eating. Stuffed peppers are on the menus at the finest Spanish restaurants, and pepper-based sauces are an integral part of the traditional food of the country.

We use peppers of all sorts and all colours – green, yellow, red and even black – sometimes fresh, sometimes dried. The sweet red *choricero* peppers from the Basque Country and Navarra; the small *ñoras* from the Levante which impart so much flavour to fish stocks; the small, very hot *romesco* peppers; and the ones, sweet or hot, used to make paprika, are the best examples of the dried varieties. The long green peppers that make the true *gazpachos* and vegetable salads, *pipirranas*, of Andalusia and the large round peppers that are prepared with stuffings in the north of Spain, Valencia or Mallorca are my favourites from around the towns, cities and homes of Iberia.

I love to serve *rosado* wines with *menestras*, young reds with pimiento dishes and oaky whites with artichokes.

CATALAN BEANS
Habas a la Catalana

I have always liked fresh broad beans when they are very small and tender. This is a hearty dish, strongly flavoured, which should be accompanied by a good red wine from Penedés.

SERVES 4

500 g (1 lb 2 oz) belly pork, rinded and halved

200 ml (7 fl oz) olive oil

1 bunch spring onions, finely chopped

450 g (1 lb) black pudding

2 kg (4½ lb) tender shelled broad beans

1 small glass dry white wine

1 bay leaf

1 sprig of mint, chopped

Salt

A pinch of sugar

½ small glass dry anis

½ small glass muscatel

Finely dice half the pork. Heat the oil in a flameproof earthenware casserole and fry the onions and the chopped pork until lightly golden. Cut half the black pudding into pieces so that it melts, add it to the pan, followed by the beans and brown for 2 minutes. Add the wine, then the bay leaf and mint. Add the remaining pudding and the remaining piece of pork, both uncut. Shake the casserole to mix, or stir with a wooden spoon. Season with salt and sugar, cover tightly and simmer gently, stirring occasionally, for about 30 minutes until the meat is cooked and the beans are tender. Add a pinch of salt and stir in the anis and muscatel before removing the casserole from the heat. Remove the bay leaf, cut the pork and black pudding into pieces, set on top of the beans and serve from the casserole.

BOTTLED PEPPERS
Pimientos en Botella

My grandmother from Navarra, which is noted for its tinned and bottled vegetables, maintained that glass jars were by far the best for preserves and in her larder she always stored lots of bottles which she would use several times a year for preserving peppers and tomatoes. She used these peppers all year round in rice dishes, cold potato and mayonnaise salads, and all sorts of dishes that call for the *morrón*, or small tinned red pepper. Bottled peppers can be stored for up to 3 months.

SERVES 4

8 red peppers

Pre-heat the oven to 180°C/350°F/Gas 4.

Place the peppers on a baking sheet and bake for 30 minutes. Place the peppers in a pan, cover with a clean cloth and leave to rest for a few minutes, then peel off the skins; they should slip off quite easily. While removing the skins, catch as much juice as you can. De-seed the peppers and slice them into thin strips. Allow to cool completely.

Put the peppers and juice in bottles, but do not overfill. Seal with cork stoppers and tie down the corks. Wrap cloths around the bottles to prevent them from hitting each other and stand them well apart in a saucepan of cold water. Bring the water to the boil and boil for 30 minutes, then remove the pan from the heat and leave to go cold before removing the bottles from the pan.

As a variation, you can substitute olive oil and crushed garlic for the pepper juice if you prefer.

STUFFED PEPPERS RIOJA-STYLE
Pimientos Rellenos a la Riojana

This recipe is made with tinned *piquillo* peppers, one of the ingredients that has emerged in recent years and caused a sensation amongst the creators of the new Basque cooking style that I admire so much. I have eaten them filled with meat, with fish, with seafood and with a mixture of different shellfish and vegetables. Sometimes they are fried, sometimes just grilled with a light cheese sauce, or even served as a salad dressed with olive oil. *El piquillo* refers to the pointed shape of these peppers which are small, fine-fleshed, succulent and, more often than not, slightly hot. The best are grown in my beloved Navarra. After these little peppers are harvested, they are roasted over wood or charcoal. When cold, they are peeled and cored to remove the seeds, then tinned or bottled. Fresh roasted peppers and other tinned varieties can also be used for this recipe.

SERVES 4

250 g (9 oz) minced pork
250 g (9 oz) minced veal
1 garlic clove, peeled and finely chopped
1 sprig of parsley, finely chopped
200 ml (7 fl oz) olive oil
4 tablespoons plain flour
A little milk

A pinch of freshly grated nutmeg
12 piquillo peppers or tinned small red peppers
3 eggs, beaten
1 glass dry white wine
4 tablespoons Tomato Sauce (see page 109)
2 tablespoons water

To make the filling, mix together the minced meats with the garlic and parsley. Heat 1 tablespoon of oil in a frying-pan and brown the meat mixture. Stir in 2 tablespoons of flour and a little milk, season with freshly grated nutmeg, and cook for 5 minutes. Stuff the peppers carefully with the filling and coat them in beaten egg, then in flour. Heat enough oil almost to cover the peppers, and fry them for about 10 minutes until cooked. Transfer them to a flameproof earthenware casserole, and keep them warm.

Make a sauce with half the oil that is left over from frying the peppers. Stir in 1 tablespoon of flour, the wine, Tomato Sauce and water. Bring to the boil and simmer for 2 minutes. Strain the sauce and pour it over the peppers. Place the casserole over a moderate heat and heat through until very hot before serving.

RED PEPPER SALAD
Ensalada de Pimientos Rojos

I have eaten this kind of salad almost everywhere in Spain, but I think that the people of La Rioja make the best ones. The reason to my mind is that they roast the peppers very carefully over the embers of great fires made at the end of the grape harvest with the wood that has been pruned from the vines in April. However, I get perfectly good results by roasting the peppers in the oven. this recipe is an excellent vegetable accompaniment to cold meats, and will keep well in the refrigerator for 2–3 days.

SERVES 4

1 kg (2 lb) red peppers
3 large garlic cloves
1 large beefsteak tomato
Coarse sea salt

4 tablespoons virgin olive oil
1 teaspoon sherry vinegar
1 sprig of parsley to garnish

Pre-heat the oven to 200°C/400°F/Gas 6.

Place the peppers, garlic and tomato in a roasting tin and bake for 15 minutes. Remove the tomato and garlic from the oven, turn over the peppers and bake for a further 15 minutes. Skin, de-seed and chop the tomato, reserving the juice. Peel the garlic. Skin, de-seed and slice the peppers, reserving the juice, and arrange the pepper slices in a serving dish.

Use a mortar and pestle to pound the garlic and tomato with some salt, or mix in a food processor. Add the oil, sherry vinegar and tomato and pepper juices and mix again. Pour the dressing over the peppers and garnish with parsley.

AUBERGINE, PEPPER
AND ONION SALAD
Escalivada

This is another of the great recipes of Catalonia and one of Spain's finest. In a version I ate recently there were medium-sized artichokes, too. This reciple calls for baking in the oven, but if you can make *escalivada* griddled over charcoal, so much the better. In its purist form *escalivada* consists only of aubergines, peppers and onions. As a variation, you can also serve *escalivada* on toast or on toasted French bread with some Catalan or Basque anchovies.

VEGETABLES

SERVES 4

*450 g (1 lb) small
    aubergines
2 red peppers
2 Spanish onions
2 large potatoes
3 tomatoes*

*4 tablespoons virgin olive oil
Salt and freshly ground
    black pepper
2 tablespoons chopped fresh
    parsley*

Pre-heat the oven to 180°C/350°F/Gas 4.

Rub all the vegetables with some olive oil. Place the aubergines, peppers, onions and potatoes on a baking sheet and bake for 45 minutes. Add the tomatoes to the baking sheet and bake for a further 15 minutes until all the vegetables are cooked. You may need to vary the cooking times depending on the size of the vegetables.

Peel all the vegetables with your fingers. De-seed the peppers and tomatoes. Tear the aubergines and peppers into thin strips, the tomatoes into pieces, and cut the potatoes and onions into rings. Arrange the vegetables on a serving dish and season to taste with salt and freshly ground black pepper. Pour the remaining oil over the vegetables, sprinkle with parsley and serve warm or cold.

POTATOES with STUFFING
Patatas con Relleno

My friend Angeles was born in Lugo, the best of the provinces of Galicia as far as good food is concerned. This is a recipe that she prepares on Sundays. It is a simple dish, but full of the character of the unique Galician peasant lore. The taste is wonderful: beneath a crispy top, the delicious centre melts with the creamy potatoes.

SERVES 4

1 kg (2 lb) potatoes
Salt
100 ml (3½ fl oz) olive oil
150 g (5 oz) tomatoes, skinned, de-seeded and halved
150 g (5 oz) Spanish onions, peeled and roughly chopped
100 g (4 oz) Serrano ham or dry-cured ham, roughly chopped
½ chicken breast, skinned and cut in pieces
25 g (1 oz) green olives, stoned
200 ml (7 fl oz) milk
2 eggs, beaten
Freshly ground black pepper

Place the unpeeled potatoes in a saucepan, just cover with salted water, bring to the boil and simmer until cooked. Drain, peel and leave to cool.

Pre-heat the oven to 180°C/350°F/Gas 4. Heat half the oil and fry the tomatoes, onions, ham, chicken and olives for 10 minutes until cooked. Chop all the ingredients finely, return to the pan and cook over a low heat until all the liquid disappears and the sauce is thick.

Meanwhile, heat the remaining oil and fry the potatoes until golden-brown. Mash the potatoes, mix with the milk and season to taste with salt. Place half the potatoes in the base of a shallow ovenproof dish, pour the sauce evenly over the potatoes and top with the remaining potatoes. Lightly season the eggs with salt and freshly ground black pepper and pour over the potatoes. Bake in the oven for 20 minutes until light golden brown and serve.

ALMANZORA POTATOES
Ajo Colorado

The cooking of the Almanzora river valley, between the provinces of Murcia and Almería, makes masterly use of the ingredients that were brought back from the New World by the conquistadores – the potato and the pepper – yet at the same time follows the Moorish culinary tradition. Just a little of the pepper flesh gives a wonderful flavour to the smooth potatoes, and imparts a richness of colour too. Dried *choricero* peppers are obtainable from Spanish or Italian delicatessens. These potatoes are usually served with little fried balls of corn.

SERVES 6

6 *dried red* choricero
  peppers
1 kg (2 lb) potatoes, peeled
  and halved
1 Spanish onion, peeled
  and halved

1 garlic clove, peeled
A few cumin seeds
100 ml (3½ fl oz) olive oil
Salt

Place the peppers in a saucepan of water, bring to the boil, then drain and repeat the process. The peppers will swell and be soft and smooth. Open out the peppers, remove the stalk and seeds and scoop out the flesh with a teaspoon. Put the pepper flesh in a saucepan with the potatoes and onion and a little water. Bring to the boil, cover and simmer until the potatoes are cooked, then drain them well, reserving some of the water. Use a mortar and pestle to pound the garlic and cumin seeds. If you have a large mortar, add the potatoes, peppers and onions and pound everything together to a thick purée. Add the oil a little at a time, pounding constantly so that the oil is well absorbed into the purée. Otherwise, you can use a food processor. When all the oil has been incorporated, thin the purée, if necessary, with a little of the reserved water, and season to taste with salt. Re-heat, if necessary, and serve hot.

Ⓥ ROAST VEGETABLE SALAD
Mojete

The word *mojete* derives from the verb *mojar*, meaning to dip. In this instance, it refers to the custom of using a piece of bread instead of a fork to help oneself to some of this delicious vegetable salad whilst waiting for the first course to arrive.

SERVES 4

750 g (1½ lb) medium-sized Spanish onions
750 g (1½ lb) red peppers
6 tablespoons olive oil
8 garlic cloves
15 g (½ oz) cumin seeds
Juice of 1 lemon
3 tablespoons white wine vinegar
Salt
2 tablespoons chopped fresh parsley to serve

Pre-heat the oven to 180°C/350°F/Gas 4.

Wrap the onions separately in kitchen foil and roast them in the oven for 45 minutes. Meanwhile, brush a baking sheet with a little oil and bake the peppers on the sheet for 20 minutes. Add 6 cloves of garlic to the baking tray, and return it to the oven for a further 10 minutes. When the vegetables are roasted, remove the foil and skin from the onions, skin and de-seed the peppers and cut them both into julienne strips. Arrange them in an earthenware serving dish.

Peel the roasted garlic and use a mortar and pestle to pound the cumin seeds, roasted garlic and the remaining peeled fresh garlic to a paste, then beat in the lemon juice, the remaining oil and the wine vinegar. Season to taste with salt. Mix well, strain and sprinkle over the *mojete* when ready. Serve sprinkled with chopped parsley.

ⓥ ONION AND POTATO OMELETTE
Tortilla Española

Together with the *cocido*, this omelette made of potato, egg and onion is one of those dishes that crosses all the regional boundaries of Spanish cooking. There are other excellent omelettes, such as the one Luis de Soto used to make with green pepper and *chorizo* but try this traditional version first.

SERVES 6

3 large old, non-waxy
   potatoes, peeled and
   diced
1 large Spanish onions,
   peeled and sliced

Salt
6 tablespoons olive oil
5 eggs, beaten

Season the potatoes and onions with salt. Heat the oil in a medium-sized non-stick frying-pan, add the potatoes and fry for a few minutes. Add the onion, cover and cook over a moderate heat for about 15 minutes, stirring from time to time to avoid browning the onion. Once the vegetables are soft and well cooked, drain off any excess oil from the pan, add the potato and onion mixture to the beaten eggs and mix well. Return the pan to the heat, pour in the egg mixture, lower the heat and shake the pan to prevent the omelette sticking. Cook on a low heat until it comes away from the sides of the pan. Remove from the heat. Turn over the tortilla by placing a plate over the frying-pan and quickly turning the tortilla upside-down on to the plate. Quickly slide it back into the pan and cook the other side for 1 minute until golden-brown. Serve hot or cold.

Ⓥ ARTICHOKES WITH ALL-I-OLI
Alcachofas con All-i-oli

Globe artichokes are a treat, and the small tender ones which
we prefer to eat in Spain are easy to prepare. It is difficult for
me to understand why there is no tradition of preparing artichokes in Britain, but I hope that this simple way to cook and
serve them with *all-i-oli* will encourage you to buy them.

The authentic Catalan and Levantine *all-i-oli* sauce contains no egg, just garlic and oil as its name implies, although I
must admit that adding egg makes the emulsion somewhat
more stable and slightly less aggressive.

SERVES 4

4 globe artichokes	3 egg yolks
2 tablespoons white wine	1 teaspoon salt
vinegar	600 ml (1 pint) olive oil
1 litre (1¾ pints) water	Juice of 1 lemon
8 garlic cloves, peeled	Freshly ground black pepper

To prepare the artichokes, use scissors to cut off the stalks
and trim off the points from the outer leaves. Spread the top
leaves and pull out the inside leaves. Scrape away the hairy
choke and place the artichokes in salted water. Bring the
vinegar and water to the boil in a large saucepan. Drain the
artichokes and add them to the pan one by one, bringing the
water back to the boil each time. Simmer for about 30
minutes, depending on the size, until tender. Drain well.

Meanwhile, blend the garlic and egg yolks with the salt in a
liquidizer. While the liquidizer is running, add the oil a little
at a time. Once the sauce has the consistency of mayonnaise,
add the lemon juice and seasoning.

SEAFOOD COURGETTES
Calabacines Marinera

This is an excellent recipe created by a friend called Fernando who lives in Guetaria. It makes a wonderful party piece as it looks tremendous with the lovely shape of the courgettes, the colour of the filling – and, of course, the delicious flavours.

SERVES 4

4 × 200 g (7 oz) courgettes
Salt and freshly ground black pepper
500 ml (17 fl oz) olive oil
450 g (1 lb) Spanish onions, peeled and finely chopped
200 g (7 oz) mushrooms, preferably wild, cut into pieces
200 g (7 oz) white fish, flaked

A pinch of freshly grated nutmeg
25 g (1 oz) fresh breadcrumbs
1 egg, beaten
100 g (4 oz) carrots, chopped
1 glass vermouth
350 ml (12 fl oz) fish stock

Peel the courgettes and put the peel to one side. Slice the courgettes in half lengthways and carefully scoop out the seeds and pulp with a teaspoon, retaining the courgette shells. Season with salt and freshly ground black pepper. Heat the oil in a frying-pan and sauté half the onions for 3 minutes. Stir in the courgette pulp and seeds, the mushrooms and the fish. Season with salt, freshly ground black pepper and nutmeg and add the breadcrumbs and egg. Simmer for 10 minutes until cooked.

Drain the oil into a clean frying-pan and sauté the

remaining onions with the carrots until light golden-brown. Add the courgette peel and sauté for 2 minutes, then add the vermouth and fish stock. Season to taste with salt and freshly ground black pepper, bring to the boil and simmer for 5 minutes. Purée the sauce in a food processor or pass it through a sieve. Pre-heat the oven to 150°C/300°F/Gas 2.

Fill the courgette shells with the fish and vegetable mixture, place in a shallow baking dish and pour over the sauce. Bake in the oven for 10 minutes.

Ⓥ TOMATO SAUCE
Salsa de Tomate

Spanish cooks always have fresh tomato sauce to use in their cooking and this is a traditional Basque way of preparing a sauce.

SERVES 4

2 tablespoons olive oil
½ Spanish onion, peeled
   and finely chopped
½ garlic clove, peeled and
   finely chopped

500 g (1 lb 2 oz) ripe
   tomatoes, skinned,
   de-seeded and chopped

Place the oil in a frying-pan and add the onion, garlic and tomatoes to the cold oil. Place over a low heat, cover and cook for 30 minutes until the oil rises to the surface. Leave to cool. Purée the sauce if you want it to be very fine.

RICE, PASTA AND COCAS

Arroces, Pastas y Cocas

Thoughts of rice conjure up in my mind childhood pictures of family Sunday lunch-time gatherings around my grandmother's table. Sometimes there were so many of us that the youngest would have to sit at a little table separate from the others, which displeased me greatly. After the starters of prawns, olives, *chorizo* and, very occasionally, Serrano ham, *La Matriarca*, as we used to call my grandmother, would bring in a huge *cazuela* filled with a delicious rice dish made with fish and shellfish and delicately coloured with saffron.

In Spain, rice has always symbolized grand communal meals of this type, at which family and friends would meet, sometimes in the open air, sometimes in people's homes. The arrival of spring, the first heat of summer, or even the autumn sun, not to mention birthdays or a stroke of luck in the national lottery, are perfect excuses, if excuses are needed, for enjoying a plate of rice.

The most widely planted cereal in the world, rice was brought to the Iberian Peninsula by the Moors in the eighth century. Now virtually a staple food, it is grown in the Ebro delta, the Valencian region and in the Andalusian lowlands. It is cooked with pulses, meat, poultry and game, vegetables, fish and even milk and sugar.

When people think of rice in connection with Spanish cooking, they usually think of the so-called *paella*, a baroque dish based on peasant food, but now created by the professional chefs, prepared as part of the family meal on Sundays, and eaten by tourists up and down the country. But of all the hundreds of rice dishes made in Spain, few are cooked in a *paella* – the flat-bottomed metal utensil which gives the dish its name – and they are not all *paellas*, which is a dry rice dish, not retaining stock as do those cooked in a *cazuela*.

If we are to talk seriously about rice dishes, we need to take a look at produce-growing and the countryside, and also at two styles of cooking: one born of the sea and the other prepared by the labourers in the inland gardens of Valencia. Spaniards would describe both styles as *cocina de aprovechamiento* – the efficient and delicious use of available ingredients.

I have eaten marvellous rices in Santander, for instance, and can recall vividly the flavour of the tiny black *chipirones* or baby squid caught by my friend's husband near Santillana del Mar. These gave the rice an extraordinary flavour and colour, gleaming and almost black, in total contrast with the white porcelain plates on which it was served. The rice dish that the charismatic Luis de Soto, a true Andalusian gentleman, used to produce once a year for the British press in Seville from a unique and idiosyncratic recipe was also memorable. I have had delicious rices in San Sebastián, too, very like the ones my grandmother used to make, and many others with Catalan names also cooked in a *cazuela*.

I must confess, however, that the most memorable I have had so far have involved Levantine traditions and cooks. The reason is that when it comes to rice in capital letters, only the people of Valencia and some of the people of Alicante really know how to spell!

If I ever had any doubts about this at all, they faded instantly one day in the kitchen of the restaurant Galbis, named after its owner, in Valencia, where I found a Japanese chef surrounded by steaming *paellas* and carefully diluting saffron in hot water. He was a sous-chef from a famous Tokyo restaurant and had been sent to Spain to learn all about the taste and techniques of our rice-cooking tradition, which produces flavours that are quite incomparable.

Galbis told me that *paella* was originally eaten in the *huerta* or vegetable garden of Valencia, during Lent, and that dried salt cod and rice were the main ingredients. Vegetables from the garden, as well as chicken, rabbit, and the snails found in the countryside soon became part of the treat. Although Galbis' *paellas* are wonderful, the speciality I most associate with the chef are the *caldosos*, a type of rice soup traditionally cooked not in the *paella* but in large earthenware pots called *pucheros*.

A good way to taste the flavours of the rice dishes of the Levante is to visit Alicante well out of the tourist season, preferably at the end of the winter, and head north. Along this stretch of the coast, fish-flavoured rice dishes and fish stews are in a class of their own. When spring is on the doorstep, the sea is usually calm, almost green and still refreshing. Around the town of Denia, there are restaurants that make exquisite rice dishes in the tradition of the local seafarers. The *calderos*, or fish stews, are described as *melosos*. Others are the *abanda* dishes, whose secret is the superb flavour the rice extracts from the stock in which it is cooked – stock made with monkfish, rascasse, eel, crab, sea bream and a host of other fish.

Moving northwards into the province of Valencia, the countryside changes once more: it is less aggressive, less beautiful, and some of it is man-made. I can see rice paddies and salt marshes in stark contrast to the fertile market gardens and the pine-tree oases which not so long ago reigned supreme. D.E. Pohren, in his book *Adventures in Taste, the Wines and Folk Food in Spain*, describes the freshwater lake of La Albufera and the small island of El Palmar: 'This lake is teeming with certain types of freshwater fish, is abundant in seasonal fowl and the surrounding marshes are renowned for their high quality rice.' Sadly, pollution has been endangering both fish and fowl, although I know that help is on its way. The Albufera and the rice paddies, however, are as beautiful as ever. The vegetables and fruit grown in this region are also exceptional. If this sounds like a gastronomical paradise, it is. If you doubt me, I recommend a quick look round Valencia's central market and all your doubts will be dispelled.

But rice is only one of the specialities of the Spanish Mediterranean. Flat, open tarts or *cocas*, known by various names throughout the region, are cooked all along this coast and in the Balearic Islands. Similar to Italian pizzas, they can be sweet or savoury, large or small, round or oval, but the dough is always made with wheat flour, olive oil, water and salt, then topped with a *sofrito* of tomato and pepper, fish and vegetables, or just sugar. Unlike the Italian pizzas, but like an *empanada*, *cocas* can also be made with a pastry topping, in which case they are known as *fasidas*. During the hot summers we spent in El Perelló when we were children, we used to buy them from the local baker for just a few pesetas.

Pasta features strongly not only in the Mediterranean region but also in the rest of the country. In Catalonia, and Barcelona in particular, pasta has a noble status. Luis Betónica, a well-known Spanish food writer, insists that pasta, like rice, did not come to Spain from Italy, but was brought by the Moors who had taken it from the Greeks.

Whatever the truth, Catalan pasta or *fideos*, which lies somewhere between vermicelli and spaghettini, is an important part of our diet. Dishes such as *cazuela de fideos con choco* made with pasta and cuttlefish, and soups made with vermicelli, *fideo fino*, or with *lluvia* (tiny 'raindrops' of pasta), or tiny star shapes, are very popular. My mother used to serve one or another of these soups every night, summer or winter, to please my father. As well as *fideos*, cannelloni is also cooked in Spain, filled with meat, cheese and vegetables, in a very similar way to the Italians.

The real difference between Catalan and Italian pasta is very well described by my son Daniel when he compares what he calls 'my grandmother's spaghetti' with mine. I cook mine *al dente*, whilst my mother cooks hers in the Catalan way: much softer and with a *sofrito* of fresh tomatoes, ham and cheese, then popped into a hot oven for a few minutes to make it crispy and impart a very special flavour.

Crisp and fruity are the *rosado* wines from Utiel or the light red wines from Valencia or Penedés which are excellent with the rice and pasta dishes of our Mediterranean coast.

GOLDEN RICE
L'Arrosseixat

This dish gets its name from the yellowish colour of the rice, and makes a tasty and substantial meal. It is typical of the whole of the Levante coastline and fishermen often make it while at sea. It works best with firm-fleshed fish and a variety of potato that will not break up during cooking.

SERVES 6

2 medium-sized Spanish
   onions, peeled
750 g (1½ lb) potatoes,
   peeled
300 ml (10 fl oz) olive oil
1 kg (2 lb) firm-fleshed fish
   (sea bream, eel, grouper),
   cut into pieces

1 teaspoon paprika
450 ml (15 fl oz) water
Salt
4 garlic cloves
550 g (1¼ lb) short-grain
   rice
600 ml (1 pint) fish stock

Cut the onions into quarters but try to leave the root intact so that they remain whole during cooking. Cut the potatoes in the same way. Heat a little oil in a large metal pan and fry the onions and potatoes over a low heat for about 10 minutes until lightly golden-brown on all sides. Add the fish and paprika and just enough water to cover the fish. Bring to the boil and season to taste with salt. Leave to simmer for about 20 minutes, depending on the type of fish, until the ingredients are cooked and the liquid has evaporated, without letting the fish and potatoes break up.

Meanwhile, slice 2 garlic cloves in half but do not peel them. Heat the remaining oil in a separate frying-pan and sauté the garlic for about 5 minutes until golden. Remove from the heat, discard the garlic and stir in the rice. Return to the heat and cook until the rice turns yellowish. Add just enough fish stock to cook the rice, but not too much as the rice grains must remain whole. Season with salt. Bring to the boil and simmer for about 10 minutes until the rice is just cooked.

Peel and crush the remaining garlic and stir in a little stock. This is called an *al-i-oli bord*. Stir this into the cooked fish.

To make the most of this dish, it is best to eat the fish first, as the rice completes cooking, to prevent the rice from becoming overdone.

SEAFOOD RICE
Arroz a la Marinera

This is a dry rice cooked in a *paella*. The secret is the exquisite stock that is traditionally made from small, cheap, but flavour-some fish. If you buy live Dublin Bay prawns, they will need to be boiled first. Drop them into a large pan of boiling salted water. Cover and bring back to the boil. Simmer over a low heat for about 10 minutes then drain and leave to cool.

SERVES 4

250 g (9 oz) monkfish, cut into pieces

1 hake's head, rinsed and dried

250 g (9 oz) prawns, preferably Dublin Bay

Salt

4 tablespoons plain flour

200 ml (7 fl oz) olive oil

1 Spanish onion, peeled and chopped

2 tomatoes, skinned, de-seeded and chopped

2 teaspoons paprika

1.2 litres (2 pints) water

2 strands saffron

250 g (9 oz) mussels, scrubbed and beards removed

4 large uncooked prawns

250 g (9 oz) squid

1 garlic clove, peeled and chopped

400 g (14 oz) medium-grain rice

Sprinkle the monkfish, hake's head and Dublin Bay prawns with salt and coat the fish with flour. Heat half the oil and fry the monkfish and hake's head for a few minutes, then remove from the pan and put to one side. Fry the Dublin Bay prawns for a few minutes then put them to one side. Peel the Dublin Bay prawns and put the tails to one side. Use a mortar and pestle or a kitchen hammer to crush the heads, shells and claws. Remove the skin and bone from the fried fish and put them and the fish to one side.

Re-heat the oil in a large pan and fry the onion until translucent. Add 1 tomato, 1 teaspoon of paprika, the water and a pinch of salt. Add the crushed Dublin Bay prawn shells and the skin and bones from the fish. Bring to the boil, cover and simmer over a medium heat for 45 minutes. Strain the stock. Crush the saffron then dissolve it in a little boiling water and add it to the warm fish stock.

Place the mussels in a saucepan with 1 cm (½ in) of water and steam over a low heat for 5 minutes, shaking occasionally, until all the shells have opened. Discard any mussels which have not opened and remove and discard the empty top shells. Strain the juices into the fish stock.

To prepare the squid (see page 59 for illustrations), pull the head and tentacles away from the body. Pull off and discard the skin. Split the body in half to remove and discard the transparent bony section. Cut the tentacles from the head just above the eye. Discard the head and cut off the beak. Wash the body and tentacles thoroughly in running water then drain and chop.

Heat the remaining oil in a 40 cm (16 in) *paella* pan, sprinkle the 4 large prawns with salt and fry them and the squid for 2 minutes. Add the garlic and remaining tomato and fry for a further 2 minutes. Add the remaining paprika and the rice, stirring rapidly. Add no more than 250 ml (8 fl oz) of the hot fish stock and season to taste with salt. Bring to the boil and cook over a high heat for 10 minutes. Add the fish and Dublin Bay prawn tails, lower the heat and simmer for a further 10 minutes. Taste and adjust the seasoning if necessary. Remove from the heat, decorate with the mussels, then cover and stand for 5 minutes before serving.

RICE WITH CLAMS
Arroz con Almejas

Rice with clams has a sensational flavour. I recommend using large French clams for this dish.

SERVES 4

1 hake's head or white fish bones	3 garlic cloves, peeled and chopped
3 carrots, peeled	1 leek, cut into julienne strips
1 Spanish onion, peeled	
750 ml (1¼ pints) water	300 g (10 oz) short-grain rice
750 g (1½ lb) large clams, scrubbed	Salt
2 tablespoons olive oil	2 sprigs of parsley to garnish

Place the hake's head or fish bones, 1 carrot, the onion and water in a large saucepan, bring to the boil, cover and simmer for 30 minutes to make a stock. Strain and reserve some flesh from the hake's head or bones.

Place the clams in a flameproof earthenware casserole with a little water. Heat for about 8 minutes until the clams open. Discard any that remain closed. Put the clams to one side and add the remaining liquid to the fish stock. Cut 1 carrot into julienne strips. Heat the oil in the *cazuela* and fry the garlic with the julienne strips of carrot and leek for 2 minutes. Add the rice and stir with a wooden spoon until the rice is coated in oil. Add the clams, hot stock and flaked fish, and season to taste with salt. Bring to the boil, reduce the heat and simmer for 25 minutes. When the rice is ready, put to one side for 5 minutes. Grate the remaining carrot and use to garnish the dish along with the parsley. Serve with red wine.

BLACK RICE
Arroz Negro

The dramatic colour of this dish can be unappealing to some people but it is a gastronomic experience, especially when made with *chipirones*, which are small, very fresh baby squid.

SERVES 4

400 g (14 oz) squid with
   their ink
100 ml (3½ fl oz) olive oil
2 garlic cloves, peeled and
   chopped
100 g (4 oz) tomatoes,
   skinned, de-seeded and
   chopped

1 teaspoon paprika
400 g (14 oz) medium-grain
   rice
1 litre (1¾ pints) hot fish
   stock
Salt

To prepare the squid (see page 59 for illustrations), pull the head and tentacles away from the body and reserve the ink sac. Pull off and discard the skin. Split the body in half to remove and discard the transparent bony section. Cut the tentacles from the head just above the eye. Discard the head and cut off the beak. Wash the body and tentacles thoroughly in running water, drain and cut into small pieces. Heat the oil in a 40 cm (16 in) *paella* pan and fry the squid for 3 minutes. Add the garlic, tomatoes, paprika and rice, stirring rapidly. When the rice becomes slightly translucent, add the hot stock and season to taste with salt. Bring to the boil and cook over a high heat for 10 minutes. Dilute the ink in a little water and add it to the pan. Gradually lower the heat and cook for a further 8 to 10 minutes until the rice is cooked. Remove from the heat and leave to stand for 5 minutes before serving.

RICE FROM ALICANTE
Arroz Abanda

This is the most delicious of the rice dishes I know, and is the quintessence of 'marine' cooking. The best versions are made in Alicante and in some parts of Castellón de la Plana. As with *arroz a la marinera*, it is the stock in which the rice is cooked that is responsible for the final quality of the dish, while the other ingredients impart a lovely reddish tinge. *Abanda* means apart, and in this context refers to the fact that the fish and potatoes are served first, followed by the rice with a little garlic and olive oil sauce.

SERVES 4

250 ml (8 fl oz) olive oil

4 medium-sized Spanish onions, peeled

4 medium-sized potatoes, peeled

½ teaspoon paprika

1.5 litres (2½ pints) water

Salt

250 g (9 oz) monkfish

500 g (1 lb 2 oz) scorpion fish (optional)

500 g (1 lb 2 oz) selection of tasty fish (such as hake, mullet, bream)

250 g (9 oz) cuttlefish or squid

100 g (4 oz) tomatoes, skinned, de-seeded and chopped

2 garlic cloves, peeled and chopped

9 strands saffron

400 g (14 oz) medium-grain rice

All-i-oli *Sauce (page 51)*

Heat 150 ml (5 fl oz) of the oil in a large casserole and fry the onions and potatoes until browned. Add the paprika, water and a pinch of salt. Bring to the boil, cover and simmer over a medium heat for about 20 minutes until the potatoes are almost cooked. Put the monkfish, scorpion fish (if using) and other fish of your choice on top of the potatoes and onions, cover, reduce the heat to a minimum and cook for a further 10–15 minutes. Remove from the heat and strain off 1.25 litres (2¼ pints) of stock. Remove the skin and bones from the fish. Arrange the fish with the potatoes and onions on a warmed serving dish and keep them warm.

Meanwhile prepare the cuttlefish or squid (see page 59 for illustrations). Pull the head and tentacles away from the body. Pull off and discard the skin. Split the body in half to remove and discard the transparent bony section. Cut the tentacles from the head just above the eye. Discard the head and cut off the beak. Wash the body and tentacles thoroughly in running water then drain and chop. Heat the remaining oil in a large *puella* pan and fry the cuttlefish or squid for 3 minutes. Add the tomatoes and garlic and fry for 2 minutes. Crush the saffron then dissolve it in a little boiling water and add it to the pan with no more than 1.25 litres (2¼ pints) of the strained fish stock. Season to taste with salt. Bring to the boil, sprinkle in the rice and cook over a high heat for 10 minutes, then gradually lower the heat and cook for a further 8 to 10 minutes. Remove from the heat and leave to stand for 5 minutes before serving.

Serve the fish with the potatoes as a first course, followed by the rice and *All-i-oli* Sauce.

PAELLA FROM VALENCIA
Paella Valenciana de la Huerta

This delicious dish has been responsible for some of the harshest criticism of Spanish food that I have heard. So much so, that I even titled one article I have written 'Beyond the Paella'. The *paella* of the much-deserved criticism, though, has little or nothing to do with the dish that is the only one with any right to bear the name, and which is made in the garden of Valencia. The best *paella* I have ever eaten was made one Sunday by a Valencian friend of mine, Tinuco, in a tiny village in Santander. The main ingredients of this rice confection are rabbit, chicken, snails and several kinds of bean. The *garrofón* or lima bean, and the *tabella* (tender beans) are delicious newly shelled, but dried ones can also be used if they have been soaked for a few hours.

SERVES 4

100 g (4 oz) lima beans
100 g (4 oz) white butter beans
100 ml (3½ fl oz) olive oil
Salt
400 g (14 oz) corn-fed chicken, cut into pieces
350 g (12 oz) rabbit, cut into pieces
125 g (5 oz) green beans, cut into pieces
100 g (4 oz) tomatoes, skinned, de-seeded and finely chopped
16 cleaned snails in their shells or a sprig of rosemary
2 strands saffron
1 tablespoon paprika
1.75 litres (3 pints) water
350 g (12 oz) short-grain rice

Unless you are using fresh beans, soak the lima beans and butter beans overnight in cold water, then drain and rinse.

Heat the oil in a 40 cm (16 in) *paella* pan with a little salt. When it is hot, add the chicken and rabbit and fry over a low heat until golden-brown. Add the green beans and fry for 5 minutes, then add the tomatoes and fry for 3 minutes. Meanwhile boil the snails (if using) in a separate pan for 5 minutes, then drain. Crush the saffron then dissolve it in a little boiling water. Add the paprika to the *paella*, quickly add the water and bring to the boil. The quantity of water is difficult to specify and may need a little practice. Add the lima and butter beans. When boiling, add the snails (or rosemary) and saffron and a pinch of salt and simmer for 30 minutes. Sprinkle in the rice and boil over a high heat for 5 minutes, then gradually turn down the heat and simmer for about 10 minutes until the rice is cooked and the liquid has evaporated.

FIDEUA

This dish is made with spaghettini, a very fine spaghetti pasta, cooked in a *paella* pan.

SERVES 4

120 ml (4 fl oz) olive oil
250 g (9 oz) uncooked langoustines
250 g (9 oz) uncooked prawns
½ teaspoon salt
250 g (9 oz) monkfish, cut into pieces
225 g (8 oz) tomatoes, skinned and cut into pieces
2–3 garlic cloves, peeled and chopped
1 heaped tablespoon of parsley leaves, finely chopped
1½ teaspoons paprika
1 litre (1¾ pints) rich fish stock
250 g (9 oz) spaghettini, broken into shorter lengths
6–8 strands saffron

For the garnish

1 lemon, cut into wedges
A few sprigs of parsley

Heat two-thirds of the oil in a large *paella* pan or large frying-pan and add the langoustines, prawns and salt. Fry evenly on both sides for 2–3 minutes then remove from the pan and put to one side. Add the monkfish to the pan and fry for a few minutes until lightly coloured on both sides.

This part of the dish can be prepared in advance if necessary. Heat the remaining oil in a separate pan and fry the tomatoes over a low heat for about 5 minutes. Pound the garlic and parsley in a mortar and pestle to make a fine *picada.* (You can use a knife to finely chop the garlic and parsley together but the texture is different.) Add this to the tomatoes with the paprika and stir well. Transfer the mixture to the monkfish in the *paella* pan. Increase the heat, add the stock and bring to the boil. Continue boiling for 2–3 minutes then add the spaghettini and bring back to the boil. Crush the saffron in a bowl then dissolve it in a little boiling water. Stir it into the pan and cook for 5 minutes. Taste the *fideua* and add salt if desired. Simmer until the spaghettini has absorbed most of the stock and is just cooked.

When you are ready to serve, arrange the shellfish on the pasta. Cover and leave to stand, allowing the heat to transfer to the seafood. Serve in the *paella* pan garnished with lemon and parsley.

FISH STEW FROM
EL MAR MENOR
Caldero al Estilo del Mar Menor

Although the fishermen of Valencia and the Mar Menor would use all kinds of fish in this moist rice dish, known as a *meloso*, some fish do tend to break down during the prolonged cooking of the stock. It is therefore a good idea to use firm-fleshed fish which hold their shape, and enable you to serve a delicious, effortless second course simply by dressing the fish with a mayonnaise or *All-i-oli* Sauce. Since some of the fish listed are rather expensive, you can vary the selection and still make a delicious dish.

SERVES 6

3 red mullet, cleaned and gutted	1 litre (1¾ pints) water
1 monkfish tail	Salt
1 John Dory (optional), cleaned and gutted	3 whiting
	500 g (1 lb 2 oz) grey mullet
1 Spanish onion, peeled and quartered	1 tablespoon olive oil
	2 red chilli peppers, de-seeded
4 garlic cloves, peeled	
1 bay leaf	350 g (12 oz) short-grain rice
500 g (1 lb 2 oz) potatoes, peeled and quartered	300 ml (10 fl oz) All-i-oli Sauce (page 51)

Place the red mullet, monkfish and the John Dory (if using), onion, 1 garlic clove, the bay leaf and potatoes in a large saucepan with just enough water to cover. Add the salt, bring to the boil, cover and simmer over a low heat for 30 minutes. Add the whiting and grey mullet and cook for a further 10–15 minutes. Heat the oil and fry the chilli peppers for 2 minutes, then crush with the 3 cloves of garlic and add them to the pan.

Remove the broth from the heat and take out the fish and potatoes. Remove the skin and bones from the fish, arrange the fish and potatoes on a warmed serving dish with a little broth and keep them warm. Strain the remaining broth, crush the pieces, rub them through a sieve and return them to the pan. Bring the broth to the boil, sprinkle in the rice and season to taste with salt. Cover and simmer for about 20 minutes until the rice is cooked. The result will be rather soupy.

Serve the rice as the first course with the *All-i-oli*, followed by the fish and potatoes.

RICE WITH YOUNG GARLIC AND SPINACH
Arroz de Ajos Tiernos y Espinacas

Whilst I have made this recipe with spring onions in Britain, I prefer to use young garlic shoots which to my taste makes the dish even more delicious.

SERVES 4–6

100 g (4 oz) dried salt cod
4 tablespoons olive oil
3 garlic cloves
10–12 young garlic shoots or spring onions, trimmed and cut in half
500 g (1 lb 2 oz) spinach, chopped

400 g (14 oz) short-grain rice
600 ml (1 pint) hot water
5–6 strands saffron
1 teaspoon paprika
Salt and freshly ground black pepper

Soak the salt cod for 24–36 hours, depending on the thickness of the pieces, changing the water at least 3 times. Drain and dry the cod and flake, discarding the skin and bones.

Pre-heat the oven to 180°C/350°F/Gas 4. Heat the oil in a flameproof earthenware dish and fry the unpeeled whole garlic (if using) until browned. Remove the garlic and put it to one side. Add the spring onions (if using) and spinach to the oil and fry over a gentle heat for 2–3 minutes, stirring. Add the cod and the rice and cook for 3–4 minutes, then add the hot water. Crush the saffron then dissolve it in a little boiling water and add it to the pan with the paprika. Season to taste with salt and freshly ground black pepper. Bring to the boil, then place in the oven for 20 minutes until the rice is cooked, taking care not to let the *paella* dry out.

PEPPER AND ONION COCA
Coca de Trempó

This is a deliciously simple *coca* from the Balearic Islands. It contains very traditional Spanish ingredients and makes a superb lunch dish served with a simple salad.

SERVES 4

1 quantity dough (page 129)
250 g (9 oz) red peppers,
   de-seeded and chopped
250 g (9 oz) tomatoes,
   skinned, de-seeded and
   chopped

250 g (9 oz) Spanish onions,
   peeled and chopped
1 tablespoon chopped fresh
   parsley
1 tablespoon olive oil
Salt

Make the dough as instructed in the recipe below.

Pre-heat the oven to 200°C/400°F/Gas 6. Mix together the peppers, tomatoes, onions and parsley and season to taste with salt. Roll out the dough to about 5 mm (¼ in) thick and curl up the edges to make a border. Place on a greased baking sheet, spread the vegetables over the dough, sprinkle with oil, season to taste with salt, and bake for 30–40 minutes until cooked through.

Ⓥ VEGETABLE COCA
Coca de Verduras

In the little town of Alella, north of Barcelona, there is a pastry shop in the main square where I could spend hours gazing through the window at the sweet and savoury *cocas*.

SERVES 4

For the dough

*200 ml (7 fl oz) hand-hot
   water*
A pinch of sugar
1½ teaspoons dried yeast
1 teaspoon salt

*250 g (9 oz) strong plain
   flour*
2 tablespoons olive oil
*1 tablespoon lard or white
   vegetable fat*

*250 g (9 oz) chard or
   spinach, shredded*
*250 g (9 oz) spinach,
   shredded*
*½ bunch spring onions, cut
   into 1 cm (½ in) pieces*
*2 tablespoons chopped fresh
   parsley*

*3 garlic cloves, peeled and
   crushed*
1 tablespoon olive oil
1 teaspoon paprika
Salt
*1 tomato, skinned,
   de-seeded and chopped*

Mix 100 ml (3½ fl oz) of water, the sugar and yeast and leave
for about 10 minutes until a frothy head forms. Mix the salt,
flour, yeast mixture, oil and lard, and add just enough of the
remaining water to mix to a soft, pliable dough. Knead well
for about 10 minutes, then place in an oiled plastic bag and
leave in a warm place to rise for about 1 hour.

Meanwhile, put the chard (if using) and spinach in a
saucepan with a very little salted water, bring to the boil and
simmer for 4 minutes. Rest for 3 minutes then drain, squeez-
ing out the excess water. Add the spring onions, parsley,
garlic and oil. Season with paprika and salt and blend well.

Pre-heat the oven to 200°C/400°F/Gas 6. Roll out the
dough to about 5 mm (¼ in) thick and curl up the edges to
make a border. Place on a greased baking tray and spread the
vegetables over the dough, sprinkle with tomato, season with
salt and bake for 30–40 minutes.

TUNA FISH EMPANADA
Empanada

Probably Galicia's favourite food, I have had round ones and square ones with dozens of different fillings, but the tuna fish *empanada* made by my friend Digna Prieto at her El Grove restaurant has to be among the best I have ever tasted. You can use fresh tuna for the filling if you prefer. This should be simmered in water with a bay leaf until cooked, then skinned and flaked.

SERVES 4

For the pastry

2 tablespoons fresh yeast	A pinch of salt
5 tablespoons tepid water	2 egg yolks
2 teaspoons sugar	A dash of anis
500 g (1 lb 2 oz) plain flour	250 ml (8 fl oz) warm milk

For the filling

2 tablespoons olive oil	400 g (14 oz) tinned tuna fish, flaked
2 large Spanish onions, peeled and finely chopped	8 strands of saffron dissolved in a little hot water
4 tablespoons Tomato Sauce (page 109)	1 egg, beaten
250 g (9 oz) tinned red peppers, chopped	

Mix the yeast and water and stir in the sugar. The water should be at blood heat. Leave in a warm place for 5 minutes until the mixture begins to froth. Mix the flour and salt in a food processor. Add the egg yolks, anis, milk and the yeast mixture and process at the lowest speed for 5 minutes.

Turn to the second lowest speed and process for a further 5 minutes until the dough is light and elastic and leaves the sides of the bowl cleanly. Remove from the bowl very gently and, using floured hands, roll into 2 balls. Cover and leave it to rise for about 30 minutes.

To make the filling, heat the oil and sauté the onions until soft. Add the Tomato Sauce, red peppers, tuna and saffron and cook for a few minutes until thoroughly combined. Preheat the oven to 200°C/400°F/Gas 6.

Roll out the dough pieces on a lightly floured surface into 2 squares. Place one on a greased baking sheet and spread with the filling, then cover with the second piece. Damp the edges and seal them together so the filling does not leak out during cooking. Roll out the trimmings very finely into long strings, and make a lattice pattern across the top. Glaze with beaten egg. Make a slit in the centre for the steam to escape and bake for 15–20 minutes until golden-brown.

FISH AND SEAFOOD

Pescados y Mariscos

I do not know whether it is good or bad to admit that Spain ranks second in the world league of lovers of fish and seafood. It depends on your point of view, and I am very conscious of the imminent problem of depletion of our seas' resources. What I am sure of, though, is that our love of fresh and salt water produce has given us one of the West's most varied and sophisticated collections of recipes for the foods from the sea. To buy fish in a Spanish market, or watch the small boats setting off early to sea or returning at sunset, is one pastime of which I never tire.

Imagine you are in a market in the north of Spain – which, save for a few differences in the species and presentation, could be anywhere in the country – and that you have paused in front of one of the stalls. It is well-lit by lamps hanging at a modest height above it, and two pretty faces ask you what you would like. The counter of the stall is angled so that you can see everything closely enough to assess the quality of what you are going to buy.

On the upper part of the stall are two wooden boxes containing fresh prawns, small and pink and almost transparent. With some rice, I could turn those into the most delicious yet simple soup for lunch. Then there are dark wicker baskets, each containing a different kind of clams: *chirlas* and *coqui-nas*. In another basket lie several kilos of oysters. At this point your mouth begins to water: it is noon, the market's finest hour, and a glass of chilled manzanilla sherry from Sanlúcar appears in your mind. Of two kinds of mussels, large and small, I would choose the smaller ones and cook them simply with onion and wine. Next you catch sight of three or four crayfish and some lobsters, still alive but with their claws bound together by elastic bands. Alongside there are decorative *cigalas* and *carabineros*, Dublin Bay and large orange prawns, which are such an intense red that they look almost artificial. There are even a few tiny Cantabrian squid, caught on a hook and line by some retired fisherman who will have brought them in early in the morning and won a good price for them. Nearby sits a box of fresh *kokotxas*, or hake cheeks, less than a kilogram in weight. I would not dare to ask how much they are, but you can be sure that they will be sold whatever the price.

On the lower part of the display, nearest to the customer, are large and small red mullet and five or six large salmon. Some are cut open, showing off their fresh orange tinge. Waving her hand at me, the fisherwoman shows me the fish's bright red gills – another sign of freshness. There are also two sizes of red mullet. Beside the salmon is a wooden box full of silver and blue sardines, so fresh that they are almost alive.

The most splendid section of the stall, looked after by the other pretty girl, who wears an embroidered apron that remains unsullied, sports what the Spaniards call serious fish: several sea bass that would cook superbly with green peppercorns, a grouper and some turbot, and the section devoted to both *pescadillas*, small hake, and other larger hake known as *merluza*.

Whether in the markets of Andalusia, or elsewhere, you

can certainly demand freshness today. Efficient methods of transportation, which when they first became available delivered all sorts of fish in perfect condition to places where only salted fish was known, now guarantee that freshness. If you are not sure about fish, I would suggest you go to the market one morning with an expert: one simple lesson will dispel your doubts for good. As a general rule, the eyes of a fresh fish are full, bold, big and shiny, rather than flat, almost opaque and whitish in colour. If the skin is dry, leave the fish where it is. As for the flesh, it should be an almost transparent white: off-white or grey are bad signs.

When there is so much choice and availability, it is difficult to talk about times of year when particular fish are at their best. However, if you happen to be in a fishing area in the spring, eat anchovy and mackerel; in the summer have plump grilled sardines, tun or *bonito*, white tuna; and at Christmas time order a good-sized, sturdy sea bream, wherever you may be.

The great variety of Spain's fish cookery can be divided into that of the fishermen; the traditional or regional as prepared by the housewife; and the innovative, as created by the great restaurateurs. All tend to adhere to certain basic principles: fresh and seasonal fish, and cooking times no longer than they need to be. Although we Spaniards may have sinned in this area in the past, tending to overcook and ruin a grand recipe or a wonderful fish, we are getting much better.

The cookery of the sea is as strong and straightforward as the men who have always practised it, and their wives who have always cooked at home in the ports. These recipes are still cooked on board the cod fleets, on the boats that fish the waters of the *bajura*, close to the coastline, and on the quayside once the catch has been unloaded.

Caldero is a substantial rice dish, and the name derives

from the vessel in which it is traditionally cooked. It is made from a good base of firm fish and a *sofrito* of fried garlic and tomatoes, then some more fish. When the fish is cooked, it is removed from the cooking liquor which is then used to cook the accompanying rice. The *ñora*, a small dried sweet pepper which is fried and ground beforehand, gives the stock its special character. The *ñora* is the ingredient that makes southern seaboard cooking distinctive, although I have also eaten similar excellent dishes of this sort in Castellón, far to the north of the land of Valencia.

Caldeirada, from Galicia, and another seaman's dish *par excellence*, differs from the *caldero* in that the fish is cooked not with rice but with potatoes, the local staple food. The potatoes are cooked in seawater and, once they have softened, the cook adds the fish he happens to have caught that day. It is usually small fish, cheap but always full of flavour. In another pan, the cook will have prepared a *sofrito* of garlic, onion, paprika, olive oil and a few drops of vinegar, which is added to the *caldeirada* just before serving. This dish jumped ship, from the fishing boat's galley to the housewife's kitchen, and is to be found today in many local restaurants.

The same happened with the most famous of all the dishes of the sea, the Basque *marmitako*. There are probably as many versions of this wonderful dish as there are sea cooks, which is a great many. Although some of the ingredients are variable, the tuna, potatoes, green peppers, olive oil and salt are common to all recipes. This dish also figures in the competitions which are part of the village fiestas to celebrate the arrival of summer. Other areas also have their own *guisos* (stews, for lack of a better term in English). Those best known by Catalan and Mallorcan fishermen are fish *suquets*. Their Canary Islands counterparts make *sancocho*, whilst in Asturias in the north they make *caldereta*.

Family and regional fish cookery is perhaps the most important in terms of the number of recipes and methods it encompasses. It is here, too, that we will find the sophisticated sauces and more precise recipes. Some dishes have evolved from fisherfolk's cooking, as is the case with the fish *zarzuelas* of Catalonia, heirs of the *suquets de peix* or fish stews, and the many Valencian rice dishes *a la marinera*. In other instances, it is the cookery born of sheer necessity, such as the many Lenten stews and the recipes based on salt fish such as *bacalao*, or salt cod, which was one of the few fish dishes that could be prepared in isolated inland regions. This is regional fish cookery at its best, and it is once again finding its way into even the most stylish Spanish restaurants.

SALT COD WITH VIZCAYAN SAUCE
Bacalao a la Vizcaína

This recipe is from my book *Life and Food in the Basque Country* and is the one I always cook at home. There are two conditions for success, and both relate to the methods of reconstituting the dry ingredients: the dried salt cod and the *choricero* red peppers.

SERVES 4

1 kg (2 lb) dried salt cod, cut into large squares

100 ml (3½ fl oz) olive oil

100 g (4 oz) Serrano ham or dry-cured ham

50 g (2 oz) belly of pork, rinded and cut into small pieces

2 large Spanish onions, peeled and chopped

1 sprig of parsley

5 dried red choricero peppers

2 hard-boiled egg yolks, dissolved in a little water

Soak the cod in cold water for 24–36 hours, depending on the thickness of the pieces, changing the water at least 3 times, then drain and rinse.

Place the fish in a large saucepan with plenty of water and heat over a very low heat for about 45–60 minutes. The temperature must be kept low otherwise the quality of the fish will deteriorate.

To prepare the sauce, place the oil, ham, pork, onion and parsley in a flameproof casserole. Bring to the boil, cover and simmer over a very low heat for about 2 hours to avoid caramelizing the ingredients. Add water to make a sauce consistency and simmer for a further 30 minutes.

Meanwhile, place the peppers in a pan and cover with water, bring to the boil, then drain and repeat the process. Spoon the flesh from the skin of the peppers. Remove the sauce from the heat and rub it through a sieve, then add the pepper flesh and egg yolks. Place the fish, skin side up, in a large flameproof dish and pour over the sauce. Heat very gently for a few minutes before serving.

BAKED SEA BREAM
Besugo al Horno

Baked sea bream is cooked on a metal grid over hot coals in northern Spain, always in the open air under an enormous canopy. The fish are cooked either whole or split open so that they cook more quickly – a perfect way for the domestic garden barbecue. If the fish is cooked whole it is then split open and the backbone removed as soon as it is ready. It can be simply dressed with some garlic and hot olive oil. In some versions of baked bream a form of paste, almost a crust, made of breadcrumbs, a little chopped onion, garlic and parsley, is used to cover the fish before putting it into the oven.

SERVES 4

2 × 1 kg (2 lb) whole sea bream, cleaned and gutted
4 tablespoons olive oil
Juice of 1 lemon

4 garlic cloves, peeled and chopped
2 sprigs of parsley, chopped
1 glass dry white wine

Pre-heat the oven to 190°C/375°F/Gas 5.

Clean the fish well, but leave the backbone in. Put the fish in an earthenware dish and cover with the remaining ingredients. Bake for 20 minutes.

RED SEA BREAM IN CIDER
Besugo a la Sidra

Charo Zapiain is the patron-chef of a wonderful cider house called Roxario in Astigarraga, just outside San Sebastián. Although this type of establishment specializes in meat and fish dishes cooked *a la brasa*, grilled, Charo always adds one or two excellent and simple recipes like this one to the menu.

SERVES 4

2 × 500 g (1 lb 2 oz) whole red sea bream, gutted, scaled and fins removed

2 tablespoons olive oil

Sea salt

3 green and red apples, cored and cut into bite-sized pieces

350 g (12 oz) shallots or small onions, peeled and quartered

1 sprig of fresh marjoram

1 teaspoon chopped fresh dill

Juice of ½ lemon

1 lemon, sliced

1 wine glass dry cider

1 sprig of fresh marjoram, without hard stems

Pre-heat the oven to 180°C/350°F/Gas 4.

Lightly score each side of the fish with a sharp knife. Brush the fish with a little olive oil and season to taste with salt. Combine the apples, shallots, herbs, lemon juice and remaining olive oil and spread evenly over the bottom of a shallow ovenproof dish large enough to hold both fish. Arrange the fish attractively on the bed of apples and shallots and place a slice of lemon on each fish. Pour the cider around the fish and bake in the oven for about 20 minutes or until the fish is cooked. Garnish with the marjoram.

GILT-HEAD IN SALT
Doradas a la Sal

Cooking *a la sal* apparently derives from the Ancient Greek custom of covering pieces of fish with mud to protect them from the intensity of the heat in their wood-fired ovens. It is one of the ideal ways of cooking the very finest fish.

This recipe is easy to make at home and can also be used for chicken. All that is needed is a deep square dish of the sort used for making lasagne or for roasting the Christmas turkey. Sea bass, sole and grey mullet, from the area of the Mar Menor in Murcia, are also cooked *a la sal*. I can assure you that the fish will not taste salty: on the contrary, it will retain its full flavour of the sea.

SERVES 4

4 × 300 g (11 oz) whole gilt-head bream

1 kg (2 lb) coarse salt

250 ml (8 fl oz) All-i-oli Sauce (page 51)

Pre-heat the oven to 200°C/400°F/Gas 6.

Wash the fish but do not gut or remove the scales. Put a layer of coarse salt in the bottom of a roasting pan. Moisten the fish with water, then place the fish on the bed of salt and cover completely with more salt. Bake in the oven for 20 minutes or until the salt begins to crack. Break open the salt crust, remove the skin and spoon out the fish straight on to the plate. Serve with the *All-i-oli* Sauce.

TROUT WITH HAM
Truchas con Jamón

Trout with ham, also called *a la Navarra*, tends to be a little greasy when served in some restaurants, so I recommend draining any excess oil on absorbent paper after frying. Trout can also be cooked without ham, just floured and fried with the garlic, parsley and lemon sauce on top, which is how they serve it in the restaurants that proliferate near the trout rivers of the Batzan valley in the Basque Pyrenees.

SERVES 4

4 × 250 g (9 oz) whole
   trout, cleaned and gutted
Salt and freshly ground
   black pepper
1 tablespoon plain flour
150 ml (5 fl oz) olive oil
250 g (9 oz) Serrano ham or
   dry-cured ham, finely
   chopped

1 tablespoon chopped fresh
   parsley
2 garlic cloves, peeled and
   finely chopped
Juice of 2 lemons
4 slices lean ham
1 lemon, sliced, to garnish

Clean the trout well and dry with a cloth. Season with salt and freshly ground black pepper and dust with flour. Heat the oil and fry the fish for about 6 minutes until cooked, then transfer them to a warmed serving dish and keep them warm.

Heat a little of the oil used to fry the fish and fry the ham, parsley and garlic until just beginning to brown, then add the lemon juice and simmer for a few minutes. In a separate pan, heat a little of the oil and lightly fry the ham slices, then wrap them around the trout. Pour the sauce over the fish and garnish with the slices of lemon.

FRESH ANCHOVIES IN VINEGAR
Boquerones en Vinagre

This is one of those recipes that even appeals to those who do not particularly love fish. Although it is sometimes difficult to get fresh anchovies, the simple temptation and marvellous results of the recipe will no doubt tempt you back to it again and again. Be careful while you are preparing the fish, as they do tend to disintegrate if not treated gently.

SERVES 4

1 kg (2 lb) fresh anchovies or sardines
250 ml (8 fl oz) white wine vinegar
1 medium-sized Spanish onion, peeled and finely chopped

8 bay leaves, crumbled
5 garlic cloves, peeled and finely chopped
1 tablespoon coarse salt
1 tablespoon fine salt
1 sprig of parsley, chopped
2 tablespoons olive oil

To prepare the fish, cut off the heads, slit along the belly of the fish and remove the guts. Remove the backbones, wash the fish under cold running water and rub the insides with a little salt to clean them. They must be absolutely clean. Drain well.

Mix together the vinegar, onion, bay leaves and garlic. Carefully arrange a first layer of fish in a dish and pour over half the vinegar mixture. Carry on arranging the fish and cover with the rest of the mixture. Add the salt and a little chopped parsley and leave them to stand overnight.

When ready to serve, remove any excess vinegar, if necessary, and add the oil and the remaining parsley.

BASQUE TUNA STEW
Marmitako

Summer is the Cantabrian tunny season, also called *albacora*. This is paler than ordinary tuna and is used to make *marmitako*, a dish that was once a Basque fisherman's delicacy called after the *marmita* or stewpot in which it was cooked. Now it is renowned throughout Spain. This particular recipe comes from the village of Ondárroa in Vizcaya.

SERVES 4 FISHERMEN!

2 tablespoons olive oil
1 Spanish onion, peeled and
    chopped
2 garlic cloves, peeled and
    chopped
1 kg (2 lb) fresh tuna, diced
1 kg (2 lb) potatoes, peeled
    and cut into medium
    sized pieces

3 green peppers, de-seeded
    and cut into medium-
    sized pieces
3 tablespoons Tomato Sauce
    (see page 109)
Salt
4 slices bread, fried

Heat the oil and gently fry the onion and garlic until golden-brown. Mix the onion and garlic with the tuna and put to one side. Mix the potatoes and peppers in a flameproof earthenware casserole and just cover with warm water. Bring to the boil, cover and simmer for about 15 minutes until the potatoes are almost cooked, then add the tuna and onion mixture and the Tomato Sauce and season to taste with salt. Bring to the boil, cover and simmer for about 8 minutes until the tuna is cooked, then add the bread slices before removing from the heat.

WHITE TUNA FISHBALLS
Albóndigas de Bonito

———

When we were children my mother often made these tasty fishballs on Fridays. I like to make them with white tuna, but you can use all sorts of fish. They are crisp and brown on the outside with a light, slightly lemony sauce.

SERVES 4

4 tablespoons olive oil
3 Spanish onions, peeled and finely chopped
3 slices stale bread, crusts removed
4 tablespoons milk
1 kg (2 lb) fresh tuna, skinned, boned and finely chopped

2 garlic cloves, peeled and finely chopped
1 tablespoon chopped fresh parsley
4 eggs, beaten
Salt
2 tablespoons plain flour

For the sauce

1 glass dry white wine
Juice of ½ lemon
25 g (1 oz) butter

1 Spanish onion, peeled and finely chopped
1 tablespoon plain flour
300 ml (10 fl oz) fish stock

Heat half the oil and fry the onions over a low heat until golden-brown. Soak the bread in the milk. In a bowl, mix the onions with the bread, tuna, garlic, parsley and 3 eggs. Season to taste with salt. Mix to a paste and form the mixture into small balls with your hands. Dust with a little flour and coat with the remaining egg. Heat the remaining oil and fry the fishballs for about 15 minutes until golden-brown.

To make the sauce, bring the wine and lemon juice to the boil and reduce by half. Melt the butter and fry the onion for about 10 minutes until golden-brown, then stir in the flour and cook for 1 minute to thicken. Stir well, then remove from the heat and leave to cool a little. Return to the heat and add the reduced wine, a little at a time, and just enough fish stock to make a light sauce. Simmer for about 15 minutes.

SEA BASS WITH TXAKOLÍ
Lubina con Txakolí

Txakolí is the wine of the Basques, but you can use a Portuguese Vinho Verde or any fresh, light and dry white wine. This is a gorgeous way of cooking sea bass. To serve the dish, arrange the julienne strips on a large serving platter, place the whole fish carefully on top and pour the pan juices over the fish. The vegetables will still be crispy and full of colour beautifully complementing the wonderful flavour of the fish.

SERVES 4

100 g (4 oz) shallots, cut into fine julienne strips
4 carrots, cut into fine julienne strips
2 leeks, cut into fine julienne strips
3 tablespoons olive oil

1.5 kg (3 lb) whole sea bass, cleaned and gutted
Salt
2 glasses Txakolí, Vinho Verde or dry white wine
1 lemon, sliced, to garnish

Pre-heat the oven to 200°C/400°F/Gas 6.

Place the vegetables in an ovenproof dish and pour over the oil. Put the bass on top of the vegetables, sprinkle with salt, cover and bake for 15 minutes. Baste with the juices, add the wine, cover and return the dish to the oven for a further 10 minutes. The fish should be slightly underdone. Arrange the vegetables on a serving platter, lay the fish in the centre, and pour over the pan juices. Serve garnished with the lemon slices.

HAKE IN GREEN SAUCE
Merluza en Salsa Verde

This is one of the pillars of Basque gastronomy and a delicious way of combining the flavours of land and sea. It is made supremely well by Gastronomic Society cooks and housewives, and the best restaurants in Spain offer it as a matter of course.

Before starting to cook, add a little sea salt to the hake and rest it in the refrigerator for a couple of hours. For this sort of recipe it is important that the oil should not get too hot as the garlic should stew rather than fry.

FISH AND SEAFOOD

SERVES 4

100 ml (3½ fl oz) olive oil

3 garlic cloves, peeled and
   sliced

4 × 150 g (5 oz) hake
   steaks

50 ml (2 fl oz) dry white
   wine

20 ml (¾ fl oz) fish stock
   or water

4 sprigs of parsley, finely
   chopped

6–8 clams, scrubbed

A few green asparagus,
   blanched (optional)

Put a flameproof earthenware casserole over an indirect heat.
Pour in the oil and when it is warm, add the garlic. Cook until
light golden, then strain the oil into a container and reserve
the garlic. Leave the oil to cool slightly, then return half of it
to the *cazuela* and set over a gentle heat. Add the fish, then
take the *cazuela* off the heat. Hold the pot with both hands
and shake constantly in a circular movement. Add the rest of
the oil little by little and shake until a thick, creamy white
sauce is achieved, add the garlic and carry on shaking the pot.
Return the pan to the heat, add the wine, stock or water and
parsley, and cook for a couple of minutes. Finally add the
clams and asparagus (if using) for a further minute. Discard
any clams that remain closed.

CATALAN FISH STEW
Zarzuela

This is a *suquet*, a Catalan fish dish which can be delicious or a disaster – it depends on where you eat it and who cooks it. *Zarzuela* is the word for a light opera in Castilian and this is, no doubt, a fish opera when cooked by the right tenor. Apart from the wonderful seafood, two of the four sauces that are the essentials in Catalan cooking are instrumental in the preparation of this dish: *sofrito* and *picada*. If you buy a live lobster, you will need to boil it first. Drop the lobster into a large pan of boiling salted water. Cover the pan and bring it back to the boil then simmer it over a low heat for 15–20 minutes. Drain and leave to cool. Live Dublin Bay prawns should be boiled in a similar way for about 10 minutes.

SERVES 6

5 tablespoons olive oil

2 Spanish onions, peeled and grated

2 ripe tomatoes, skinned, de-seeded and finely chopped

2 thin slices bread, crusts removed

4 almonds, toasted and skinned

2 garlic cloves, peeled and chopped

1 × 400 g (14 oz) cooked lobster

200 g (7 oz) squid

4 cutlets monkfish

4 cutlets halibut

Salt

1 tablespoon plain flour

4 uncooked prawns

4 Dublin Bay prawns (or 4 more uncooked prawns)

16 mussels, scrubbed and bearded

8 large clams, scrubbed

1 tablespoon chopped fresh parsley

1 glass Spanish brandy

Heat 3 tablespoons of oil and fry the onions over a low heat, adding a few drops of water during the cooking process. When the onions are lightly golden, add the tomatoes and cook until the oil separates and appears at the top, then put to one side. This is the *sofrito*. Heat a little more oil and fry the bread. Place in a mortar with the almonds and 1½ cloves of garlic and pound together to a fine paste or *picada*. Put to one side.

To prepare the lobster, split it in half lengthways. Remove and discard the intestinal vein which runs down the tail.

To prepare the squid (see page 59 for illustrations), pull the head and tentacles away from the body. Pull off and discard the skin. Split the body in half to remove and discard the transparent bony section. Cut the tentacles from the head just above the eye. Discard the head and cut off the beak. Wash thoroughly in running water then drain and slice.

Season the monkfish, halibut and lobster with salt and dust with a little flour. Heat a little oil and brown the fish separately: monkfish, halibut, lobster, then the squid, prawns and Dublin Bay prawns. As they are cooked, drain the fish and arrange them in a large flameproof earthenware dish. Add the mussels and clams. Add the remaining garlic and the parsley and stand the dish over a low heat. Pour over the brandy and flambé. Pour in the *sofrito*, just cover with hot water, bring to the boil and simmer for 4 minutes until the clams and mussels have opened. Discard any that remain closed. Mix in the *picada* and season to taste with salt. Cook for a further 5 minutes and serve immediately.

POULTRY AND SMALL GAME
Aves y Caza

The author of a treatise on cooking published in Spain in 1894 stated that only in the Cordon Bleu, a luxury shop in the Calle de Barquillo in Madrid, would you be able to buy fine birds of all descriptions, dead or alive, the latter being in the best of health, and all having been raised on the very best feed. Even when I was a child, chicken, capon and turkey were still comparatively unusual and were only cooked at Christmas and on certain feast days.

These days, however, poultry in general and chicken in particular are part of everyday family eating. They can be birds bought in the local supermarket, the municipal market's specialist *pollería huevería* or chicken and laying hen shop, or farmyard birds destined to be turned into a delicious stew.

Wherever they are bought, we always use corn-fed chicken or fowl in Spanish cooking. A corn diet imparts an orangey-yellow colour to the flesh and makes them more appetizing than the slightly anaemic-looking specimens bought by the rest of Europe. Sadly, now that we are one of Europe's glorious Twelve, these pale creatures have already begun to appear in Spanish shops. I can see implict danger signs on them for the quality of our cooking.

Way back in rural Spain, there were few labourers' households that did not raise their own chickens and a duck or two. The tiny chickens we call *tomateros* have always been much appreciated, and in places like Galicia they used to roast capon, on special occasions, in the village baker's oven. This is not purely a practice of the north-west. I remember that in El Perelló, a village in Valencia where we used to spend the summer when I was young, my mother would send the *cazuelas* of rice and chicken she had prepared to be cooked in the local oven, and we would collect it on our way back from the beach.

Rabbit and hare also play an important part in the cooking of many areas in the Peninsula. The mother of a very good friend of mine lived in Falset, a village in the province of Tarragona, and she used to cook the most extraordinary recipes with farmyard rabbit which she claimed – and I have to agree – was far more tender and tasty than the rabbit her husband used to bring down occasionally from the mountains. She cooked it in a chocolate sauce, or with *romesco* sauce.

The genuine *paellas* that the field workers used to have for lunch were also made with rabbit or other animals caught during the men's long hours labouring, as are the *gazpachos* of La Mancha in central Spain, and in the inland areas of the Levante. These bear no relation to the Andalusian *gazpacho*: but instead contain up to five different kinds of meat, including rabbit, partridge, wood pigeon and chicken, plus a kind of unleavened bread.

During the open shooting season, goose and duck, both farmyard and wild, are cooked in innumerable ways. Some of these are particularly interesting. The Catalans cook goose with pears or figs, or stuffed with apples, and in the area of La Selva in Gerona they serve it with salsify. In Andalusia I have

also eaten excellent duck cooked *a la sevillana* (Seville-style), with olives, and in Jerez, extraordinarily good wild duck cooked with a vegetable sauce.

I always associate partridge, quail and pheasant dishes with the meals one of my father's sisters used to produce. Her husband was a great lover of shooting who would frequently take his dogs with him on shooting expeditions in the fields around Ocaña and Aranjuez in Toledo. I also associate these birds with some of my Navarrese grandmother's recipes for she used to make a dish of quail with very young tender beans, *pochas*, that I consider to be one of the best in Spain.

As far as the more specialized game-bird dishes are concerned, such as those for woodcock and guinea fowl, for example, it has been the *Nueva Cocina* Spanish chefs who have managed to learn to cook and present them correctly, as well as giving them their rightful place on restaurant menus. There are now hundreds of recipes for these birds: young farm pigeon filled with truffles, guinea fowl thighs with wild mushrooms, farmyard duck cooked in honey and rosemary, and the incredible pheasant bread that Juan Mari Arzak makes in his restaurant in San Sebastián. These are just a few examples of the cooking I have been fortunate enough to relish over the last decade, a period that has seen Spanish gastronomy enjoy a marked renaissance.

CHICKEN IN BEER
Pollo a la Cerveza

We Spaniards like beer, and I love a *caña*, a glass of draught beer, in the middle of a hot summer's day. I do like to use beer as an ingredient, too. In this recipe, it marries perfectly with the sweet and sour flavour of the brown sugar, vinegar and the trilogy of herbs that I use most in my own cooking: thyme, rosemary and a bay leaf. This recipe also includes tiny mushrooms, tossed briefly in the frying-pan and added towards the end of the cooking time. Together with the fried bread, they create a very attractive looking dish.

SERVES 4

8 tablespoons olive oil

12 corn-fed chicken drumsticks

½ garlic clove, peeled and chopped

½ medium-sized Spanish onion, peeled and chopped

1 large can lager

1 teaspoon soft brown sugar

1 teaspoon sherry vinegar

1 bay leaf

1 teaspoon chopped fresh rosemary

1 teaspoon chopped fresh thyme

Salt and freshly ground black pepper

100 g (4 oz) button mushrooms

4 slices bread, halved

Heat half the oil in a frying-pan and fry the chicken pieces and garlic until lightly browned. Add the onion and sauté for 1 minute. Transfer the chicken to a metal dish. Pour the beer into the frying-pan and bring to the boil, scraping up all the meat juices, then pour the beer over the chicken. Add the sugar, sherry vinegar and herbs, and season to taste with salt and pepper. Bring to the boil, cover and simmer gently for about 30 minutes until the chicken is tender.

Meanwhile, heat a little of the remaining oil in a frying-pan and quickly toss the mushrooms in the oil for a few minutes. Add them to the chicken. Heat the remaining oil and fry the bread until crisp, then serve with the chicken.

CHICKEN WITH TOMATO AND PEPPERS
Pollos al Chilindrón

One way that chicken and lamb are cooked in the region of Aragón in the north-east of Spain is called *chilindrón*. The sauce is made from tomatoes, peppers, garlic and onions. Luis Miguel Vergara, of the Bar Cariñena in the village of the same name in Zaragoza, insists that *chilindrón* should be made with small peppers and little garlic and served with one of the robust wines made in his part of the world. This is a good recommendation, as the dish cooks to a delicious and colourful rich sauce with just a hint of spiciness.

SERVES 4

250 ml (8 fl oz) olive oil
2 × 600 g (1 lb 5 oz) poussins, jointed (see page 156)
4 large tomatoes, skinned and chopped
4 small green peppers, de-seeded and chopped

1 large Spanish onion, peeled and chopped
2 garlic cloves, peeled and chopped
1 teaspoon chilli powder
150 g (5 oz) ham, thinly sliced and cut into pieces
1 glass dry white wine
Salt

Heat a little oil and fry the chicken pieces until golden-brown and cooked through. Transfer them to a warmed serving dish and keep them warm. Heat the remaining oil and fry the tomatoes, peppers, onion, garlic and chilli powder over a low heat for 5 minutes. Add the ham and wine and cook for a further 5 minutes. Season to taste with salt, and serve with the chicken.

ROAST CHICKEN WITH PINE KERNELS AND RAISINS
Pollo al Horno con Piñones y Pasas

Until a few years ago, the only chickens eaten in Spain were fed on corn so they were a more appetizing colour than the pinkish or whitish ones which are usually available in Britain. I recommend using corn-fed chicken rather than the free-range ones available now in British supermarkets, which are just as delicious but tend to be a bit dry. My oven often sees chicken prepared in this way because it is so simple and the flavour achieved so delicate.

SERVES 4

1 × 1.5 kg (3 lb) corn-fed chicken
Salt and freshly ground black pepper
1 tablespoon olive oil
15 g (½ oz) butter

75 g (3 oz) raisins, soaked for 30 minutes then drained
75 g (3 oz) pine kernels
1 glass dry oloroso sherry

Pre-heat the oven to 200°C/400°F/Gas 6.

Season the chicken with salt and pepper and brush with oil. Roast in the oven for about 1½ hours until brown and tender, basting occasionally. Transfer to a warmed serving dish. Heat the butter and fry the raisins and pine kernels for 4 minutes. Add them to the chicken, pour over the sherry and set alight to serve.

1

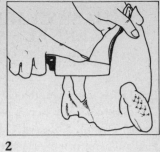

2

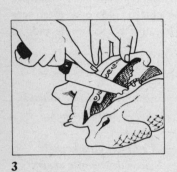

3

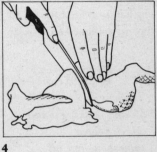

4

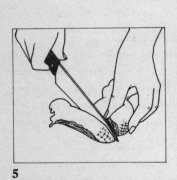

5

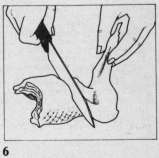

6

FARMYARD CHICKEN
FROM JEREZ
Gallo de Campo a la Jerezana

This recipe is from José Antonio Valdespino of Jerez. It is delicious served with a light purée of potatoes and milk.

SERVES 6

1 × 2.5 kg (5½ lb) corn-fed chicken

150 ml (5 fl oz) olive oil

1 garlic clove, peeled and chopped

1 kg (2 lb) Spanish onions, peeled and sliced

2 green peppers, de-seeded and sliced

Salt and freshly ground black pepper

½ bottle good-quality dry oloroso sherry

350 ml (12 fl oz) chicken stock

50 g (2 oz) pine kernels

50 g (2 oz) sultanas

Joint the chicken by first cutting through the parson's nose (1), then stand the chicken in a vertical position (neck end down). Insert the knife into the cut you've made, and cut straight down the back of the chicken (2). Place it skin-side down, open it out flat, and cut right through the breastbone (3). Now turn the 2 halves of the chicken skin-side up, stretch out the leg as far as you can, and cut through the natural line dividing the leg from the breast (4). Then find the thin white line at the centre of the joint, and cut through it (5). For 8 portions cut the breast portion in half (6).

Heat the oil in a large frying-pan and add the chicken and garlic. Fry until dark golden, then transfer to a flameproof earthenware casserole. Sauté the onions and peppers in the oil until well browned, then add them to the chicken with the oil. Place over a medium heat and, when the temperature is fairly high, season to taste with salt and pepper. Add the sherry and simmer until it has reduced by half. Add the stock, bring to the boil, then lower the heat, cover and simmer for about 30 minutes until tender. Remove the chicken, cut it off the bone into very small fillets and arrange on a serving plate. Meanwhile strain or blend the sauce and return it to the heat to reduce a little more. Pour the sauce over the chicken and sprinkle over the pine kernels and sultanas.

CAPON WITH OYSTERS
Capón con Ostras

I have always thought it a shame to cook oysters because all I need is for someone to pull them out of the sea and open them for me so that I can just squeeze a little lemon juice over them and eat them. This recipe, however, is the exception that proves the rule. It comes from Lugo, a province of Galicia.

SERVES 4

8 oysters, scrubbed
100 ml (3½ fl oz) pork or chicken fat
100 g (4 oz) veal, minced
500 g (1 lb 2 oz) mixed vegetables, peeled and chopped
6 eggs, beaten
A pinch of freshly grated nutmeg

Salt and freshly ground black pepper
100 g (4 oz) lard, melted
1 × 2 kg (4½ lb) corn-fed chicken
Juice of 1 lemon
300 ml (10 fl oz) chicken stock
4 slices bread

Pre-heat the oven to 190°C/375°F/Gas 5.

Shell the oysters over a fine strainer set in a bowl to catch the juice. Hold the oysters with the rounded shell up and slide a sharp knife into the hinge. Twist the knife to prise the hinge open and cut the muscles above and below the oyster. Run the knife between the shells to open them and cut away the oysters.

Heat the fat and fry the veal and most of the oysters for about 5 minutes until half cooked. Meanwhile, cook the vegetables in boiling salted water for 5 minutes, then drain. Add the vegetables to the meat with 4 eggs and mix well. Add the nutmeg and season to taste with salt and pepper. When the mixture has absorbed all the fat, remove from the heat and mix well, then add the remaining eggs and oysters and a little of the oyster juice.

Season the chicken with salt and pepper and brush it with a little melted lard. Stuff the chicken with the veal and oyster mixture and place it on a spit roast or on a grid in a roasting tin. Cook in the oven for about 1½ hours until the chicken is tender, draining and reserving the meat juices occasionally. Heat the meat juices with the lemon juice and stock to make a sauce.

Just before the chicken is ready, heat the remaining lard and fry the bread until golden-brown. Arrange the bread on a warmed serving dish. Cut the chicken into pieces and arrange on top of the bread. Cover with the stuffing and pour over the sauce.

CHICKEN IN SANFAINA SAUCE
Pollo en Sanfaina a la Catalana

Sanfaina is true Mediterranean food, at its best at the end of summer when the tomatoes are full of flavour. Use a dry young wine from the region of Penedés to cook the sauce and accompany the dish.

SERVES 4

2 Spanish onions, peeled
5 tablespoons olive oil
1 × 1.5 kg (3 lb) corn-fed
    chicken, cut into 8 pieces
    (see page 156)
100 g (4 oz) ham, diced
1 green pepper, skinned, de-
    seeded and cut into strips
1 red pepper, skinned, de-
    seeded and cut into strips
2 aubergines, cut into strips
1 garlic clove, peeled and
    chopped
1 bay leaf
1 sprig of thyme
1 sprig of parsley
200 g (7 oz) tomatoes,
    skinned, de-seeded and
    chopped
250 ml (8 fl oz) chicken
    stock
1 glass dry white wine
Salt and freshly ground
    black pepper
4 slices bread, cut into
    triangles
1 tablespoon finely chopped
    fresh parsley

Chop 1 onion finely and slice the other into rings. Heat 4 tablespoons of oil in a large flameproof casserole. Fry the chopped onion for 1 minute, then add the chicken pieces, ham, peppers, aubergines and garlic. Tie the bay leaf, thyme and parsley into a bouquet garni. Add to the pan and fry until the chicken is lightly browned. Increase the heat and cook for about 10 minutes, but do not allow the ingredients to burn. Add the tomatoes, onion rings, stock and wine. Season with salt and pepper. Bring to the boil, then reduce the heat, cover and simmer for a further 20 minutes until the chicken is cooked. Remove the bouquet garni.

Heat the remaining oil and fry the bread until golden-brown. Garnish the chicken with the fried bread and parsley.

CHICKEN LIVERS WITH ONION
Higaditos Encebollados

Children who normally refuse to eat liver usually like it prepared in this way. The onions should be cut into very thin slices and cooked slowly to prevent them burning, while allowing them to caramelize. The livers are added at the last minute as they need only a short time in the pan to cook.

SERVES 4

6 tablespoons olive oil
4 large Spanish onions, sliced into thin rings
2 small glasses palo cortado sherry or dry Amontillado

1 kg (2 lb) chicken livers, thinly sliced
Salt and freshly ground black pepper

Heat the oil in a large, heavy-based saucepan. Add the onions and cook over a low to moderate heat for about 20 minutes, stirring occasionally, until soft and golden. Stir in the sherry and cook for a few minutes to allow time for the nutty flavour to develop. Heat a frying-pan. Drain most of the oil and sherry from the onions into the hot pan, add the liver and sauté for 2 minutes, stirring gently, then transfer them to the pan with the onions and continue to cook for 1–2 minutes. Season to taste with salt and pepper and serve immediately.

OLD ANDALUSIAN CHRISTMAS TURKEY
Pavo Navideño Andaluz

I remember that the first time I spent Christmas with my husband's family on the Isle of Wight, Charles, my father-in-law, asked me if we had turkey for Christmas in Spain. In fact, this bird reached the rest of Europe via the conquistadores who brought it back from the Americas to Spain, replacing pigeon which had been the Moslems' and Jews' festive dish. Even today, in the countryside and many of the towns of Andalusia, it is still cooked for dinner on 24 December, almost exactly as pigeon was prepared centuries ago. This recipe ensures that the turkey remains moist and tasty, subtly flavoured by the fresh herbs.

SERVES 10

150 ml (5 fl oz) olive oil
1 large turkey, jointed (see page 156)
1 Spanish onion, peeled and chopped
2 sprigs of thyme
2 sprigs of rosemary
1 bay leaf
3 strands saffron
3 sprigs of parsley, finely chopped
Salt and freshly ground black pepper

Heat the oil in a deep flameproof earthenware casserole and sauté the turkey pieces for about 15 minutes until well browned. Transfer to a separate dish. Add the onion, thyme, rosemary and bay leaf to the casserole and fry for about 10 minutes until the onion is golden. Return the turkey pieces to the pot and stir everything together over the heat for a couple of minutes, then just cover with water. Crush the saffron, then dissolve it in a little boiling water and add it to the pan with the parsley. Bring to the boil then reduce the heat and season to taste with salt and pepper. Cover loosely and simmer for about 2 hours until the turkey is tender and the liquid has reduced by more than half to form a smooth sauce. If the sauce is not thick enough, remove the lid and boil to reduce the liquid a little further.

QUAILS BRAISED WITH GRAPES
Codornices Braseadas con Uvas

I can still remember helping my grandmother to pluck the feathers from these fowl. She would singe the quail on a lively flame, and let me pluck out the little feathers that had been left behind by this ostentatious operation. Today, small quail can be bought ready plucked so her recipes are easier to make, but because these are farm birds they do not have quite the delicious flavour of the birds that are free to flutter about the countryside. In the summer, I prefer quail simply wrapped in a few rashers of bacon and barbecued. However, this is an excellent, what I call a 'Saturday evening', recipe, which is when we gather friends around our table.

SERVES 4–6

8 quails
8 slices streaky bacon
175 g (6 oz) spring onions,
    chopped
175 g (6 oz) mushrooms,
    chopped
2 small carrots, peeled and
    chopped
1 Spanish onion, peeled and
    chopped
75 g (3 oz) butter
1 tablespoon lard or bacon
    fat

250 g (9 oz) grapes,
    preferably moscatel,
    skinned and de-pipped
4–5 black peppercorns
A pinch of freshly grated
    nutmeg
250 ml (8 fl oz) dry white
    wine
120 ml (4 fl oz) Spanish
    brandy
2 garlic cloves, peeled and
    crushed

Pre-heat the oven to 190°C/375°F/Gas 5.

Place the quails, each with a slice of bacon over the top, in a large ovenproof dish without overlapping them. Add the vegetables. Melt the butter and lard or bacon fat, and pour it over the quails and vegetables. Cook in the oven for 15 minutes until the bacon browns and it starts to sizzle.

Meanwhile, use a mortar and pestle to pound half the grapes, the peppercorns and nutmeg. Blend with the wine and brandy. Mix in the garlic and pour this over the quails. Cook for a further 30 minutes, basting occasionally. Add the rest of the grapes. Drain all the juice into a saucepan and bring to the boil to reduce slightly. If the sauce is too thin, mix a spoonful of flour with some cold water and add it to the sauce, allowing it to cook for a few more minutes. Arrange the quails, bacon and vegetables on a serving dish, pour over the sauce and serve.

PARTRIDGES
MADRID–BARCELONA STYLE
Perdices Madrid–Barcelona

The Madrid–Barcelona restaurant, in the Catalan capital, is one of those places where time seems to have stood still and you find yourself transported back to the 1930s. It is not only the décor but also the way the waiters move around the tables. I shared this incredible dish with my friend Claudia Roden one spring when we were both working in that beautiful Mediterranean city. The chef at this excellent restaurant let me have his recipe.

SERVES 4

6 small Spanish onions, peeled and chopped
2 carrots, peeled and chopped
2 tomatoes, skinned, deseeded and chopped
6 garlic cloves, peeled and chopped
50 g (2 oz) mushrooms, chopped
2 gherkins, chopped
4 partridges
250 ml (8 fl oz) meat stock
300 ml (10 fl oz) olive oil
150 ml (5 fl oz) red wine vinegar
1 bay leaf
1 teaspoon chopped fresh thyme
1 teaspoon paprika
Salt and freshly ground black pepper

Pre-heat the oven to 160°C/325°F/Gas 3.

Place the vegetables and partridges in a flameproof casserole. Add the stock, oil, wine vinegar, bay leaf, thyme and paprika, and season to taste with salt and pepper. Bring to the boil and cover tightly. Transfer to the oven for 1½–2 hours until the partridges are cooked and the vegetables are tender.

Partridges in Vinaigrette

You can also cook partridges by sealing them in a little oil. Next fry julienne strips of onion in the same oil until they are about to brown, then return the partridges to the pan with 500 ml (17 fl oz) olive oil. Simmer or cook in the oven, as above, and flavour the partridges with 250 ml (8 fl oz) red wine vinegar, salt and freshly ground black pepper just before they are ready to serve.

PARTRIDGES WITH CHOCOLATE SAUCE
Perdices con Chocolate

Some recipes from Navarra and Catalonia use chocolate as a special ingredient in their sauces. One classic example is the Costa Brava dish known as *mar y montaña*, or sea and mountain, which contains lobster and chicken. Another is this recipe from my grandmother's notes. Though the combination of chocolate and savoury foods sounds risky, the results are surprisingly delicious – believe me!

SERVES 4

16 baby onions
2 partridges, halved
Salt and freshly ground black pepper
2 tablespoons plain flour
4 tablespoons olive oil
2 sticks celery, cut into strips

600 ml (1 pint) chicken stock
2 tablespoons white wine vinegar
1 bay leaf
4 slices stale French bread
100 g (4 oz) bitter chocolate, grated

166

Place the onions in boiling water for 1 minute, then drain and peel, leaving them whole. Season the partridges with salt and pepper, and dust them with flour. Heat a little oil in a flameproof earthenware casserole and fry the partridges and onions until lightly browned, stirring occasionally. Add the celery and cook for 2 minutes, then stir in the stock, wine vinegar and bay leaf. Cover and simmer for 45 minutes.

Heat the remaining oil until very hot. Fry the bread until brown, then drain on kitchen paper and place on a serving plate. Remove the partridge halves from the sauce and place one on each piece of fried bread. Garnish with the celery and onions. Remove the bay leaf and bring the sauce to the boil. Check and adjust the seasoning if necessary and add most of the chocolate. Once the chocolate melts, it thickens the sauce instantly. Add a little more chocolate if necessary. Pour the sauce over the partridges and serve.

RABBIT IN SALMOREJO
Conejo al Salmorejo

As well as the cold soup made in Córdoba, the word *salmorejo* refers to a sauce that is made in the Canary Islands from olive oil, vinegar, salt and pepper and shows undoubted Andalusian or Moorish influence. There can be nothing more pleasant than to savour this dish in the sunshine of the Islands' gentle winter. The rabbit is cooked until tender, crisp and golden, and topped with an unusual and tasty sauce. It is traditionally served with *papas arrugadas* which is a dish of potatoes boiled in heavily salted water until they are soft, the water poured off and the potatoes cooked again over a very low heat until they are slightly wrinkly.

SERVES 4

1 rabbit, cut into 8–12 pieces	*2 small chicken or rabbit livers*
250 ml (8 fl oz) olive oil	*1 green pepper, de-seeded and roughly chopped*
1 garlic clove, peeled and chopped	*A pinch of ground cumin*
1 bay leaf	*1 teaspoon paprika*
1 sprig of thyme	*1 teaspoon sherry vinegar*
Salt	*1 tablespoon water*

Place the rabbit in a bowl with half the oil, half the garlic, the bay leaf, thyme and a pinch of salt. Marinate for 2 hours, turning occasionally, then remove from the marinade.

Reserve 1 tablespoon of oil. Heat the remainder and fry the rabbit pieces for about 20 minutes until golden-brown and cooked through. Drain and place on a warmed serving plate, keeping them warm.

Meanwhile, boil the chicken or rabbit livers in a little salted water for about 8 minutes until cooked, then drain them. Transfer them to a mortar or food processor with the remaining garlic, the green pepper, cumin and paprika, and pound or process to a thick sauce. Thin the sauce with the sherry vinegar, water and remaining oil, and season with salt. Pour the sauce over the rabbit and serve immediately.

DUCK BREAST WITH APPLE
Pechuga de Pato con Manzanas

This is a creation of the New Basque cookery which I tasted with relish in a Madrid restaurant.

SERVES 4

1 kg (2 lb) duck or chicken
    bones

1 Spanish onion, peeled and
    sliced into julienne strips

1 leek, cut into julienne
    strips

1 carrot, cut into julienne
    strips.

500 ml (17 fl oz) dry white
    wine

500 ml (17 fl oz) water

Salt and freshly ground
    black pepper

2 teaspoons arrowroot
    (optional)

1 tablespoon water
    (optional)

2 green apples, Reineta if
    possible, peeled, cored
    and cut into 6

50 g (2 oz) butter

4 duck breasts

A little pork fat

8 small slices of fresh duck
    or chicken liver

4 sprigs of mint to garnish

Pre-heat the oven to 200°C/400°F/Gas 6. Put the bones and vegetables in a flameproof earthenware pot and brown in the oven for 15 minutes. Add the wine and water and place the pot on the hob. Bring to the boil, cover and simmer for 30 minutes. Remove the bones from the dish and boil until the liquid has reduced by half. Strain the sauce and season to taste with salt and pepper. If the sauce is not thick enough, mix the arrowroot and water and stir it into the sauce over a low heat for 2 minutes until the sauce thickens. Keep the sauce warm over a bain-marie of hot water.

Blanch the apples in boiling water for just a few seconds, then drain. Heat the butter and sauté the apples for 2 minutes until they are golden. Remove from the pan and keep warm.

Season the duck breasts with salt and pepper, and place in a casserole with the pork fat. Put in the oven for 25 minutes, then slice the duck into thin fillets and put to one side. Fry the liver lightly in the same pan. Arrange some apple, duck and liver on each plate, cover with a little sauce and garnish with mint.

DUCK WITH PEARS
Pato con Peras

This is my, somewhat lighter, version of the goose dish they make in the Ampurdán region of Gerona, in my opinion one of Catalan gastronomy's most interesting areas. The original recipe includes cream or milk and pork fat, for which I substitute oil from Borjas Blancas, Lérida, which is very low in acidity and of an exquisite flavour. The recipe is usually cooked in the oven, although I prefer to cook it on the stove, where I have more control over the ingredients.

SERVES 4

4 tablespoons olive oil
1 duck, cut into 8 pieces
2 Spanish onions, peeled and chopped
1 carrot, peeled and chopped
2 ripe tomatoes, skinned and chopped
1 stick cinnamon
1 teaspoon chopped fresh thyme

250 ml (8 fl oz) chicken stock
1 garlic clove, peeled
10 almonds, toasted and skinned
1 glass Spanish brandy
Salt
8 green pears, peeled, cored and halved

Heat half the oil and fry the duck until well browned. Put to one side. Add and heat the remaining oil and fry the onions, carrot, tomatoes, cinnamon and thyme until the onions are soft. Add the stock and bring to the boil, cover and simmer for 30 minutes. Remove the cinnamon stick and purée the sauce in a food processor or rub it through a sieve, then return it to the pan with the duck and re-heat. Use a mortar and pestle to pound the garlic and almonds to a paste, then mix in the brandy. Add this to the sauce and season to taste with salt.

Meanwhile, place the pears in a saucepan and just cover with water. Bring to the boil and simmer for 5 minutes, then drain and mix the cooking liquor into the sauce.

Arrange the duck pieces on a warmed serving place and pour over the sauce. Decorate with the pears and serve at once.

MEAT AND LARGE GAME
Carne y Caza

O ne day I asked my butcher for two large ribs of beef chops, one of ox meat, which to me is the tastiest of all, and one of *ternera mayor*, the older veal we love in Spain. That night I had arranged to go with a group of friends to the Sidrería Rosario, a cider house where, as is the custom in the north of Spain, they give you as much cider as you can drink and cook your meat for you, charging 400 pesetas each.

Whilst the butcher was wrapping the meat in grey paper, I was already thinking about the great grill that would be placed over beech-wood charcoal, which is how we like to roast this kind of meat in some areas of Spain. We put the meat on the grill and, by the time the charcoal's blue flames began to wane and the fire had coaxed the meat to a gentle sizzle, our taste-buds were almost exploding with delight. By this time, the meat was ready and it was whisked on to the plate. Slightly caramelized on both sides yet still pink in the middle, it was cooked to perfection. Little else was needed at the table, just knives and forks, good bread and full-bodied Reserva wine from Rioja. I would always eat meat this way if I could.

But that would overlook classic meat cookery from other regions. The Castilians love roast meat, especially in Segovia and the environs of the Duero river as it winds its way across the *meseta*. This plateau of Castile is not, however, a country of splendid cattle and green bucolic scenery: Castile is arid, yet very beautiful, and its wealth lies in the winter and summer pastures that support its flocks of sheep. Suckling pig, kid and the tender meat of young lambs are roasted in huge wood-fired ovens inherited from the Romans and perfected by the Moors. In these ovens, the meat cooks for only a short time at very high temperatures. It comes out brown and crisp on the outside, tender and succulent on the inside. Lamb is usually dressed with herbs, spices, oil and vinegar, but suckling pig is served just as it is.

There are many areas in Spain, however, where the tradition of eating little meat, especially beef, still holds true. In Galicia, for example, the superb local meat has only ever been eaten on grand occasions, or at family meals as part of a rich hotpot, or as a well-tried but boring fillet with fried potatoes. Yet its quality is such that in the markets of Madrid it is often the most expensive meat on show, labelled with a little card explaining that 'this is from Galicia'.

During one summer I spent with my son Daniel in the little village of Lozoya near Madrid, I had to bring meat out from the capital once a week. In the local grocery shop the only ingredient ever seen, apart from country produce, was the occasional piece of meat brought once a month from the nearest village. This was the only opportunity of making a change from the chicken or wild rabbit caught by the locals, children or adults. And I am talking about only seven or eight short years ago.

This is not true of all areas, however, and among the meat dishes that remain clearest in my memory is a superb stew with olives that I had in the Río Grande restaurant in Seville after a week of eating only fish and seafood on the coast. This restaurant has the best views in the city, and on its menu are two other things that are to be recommended: the extraordinary Jabugo ham, and the bull's tail which they cook almost as well as in Córdoba where they are true masters of this dish.

The Spaniards are fond of lamb and veal, although veal in Spain is quite different to the veal eaten in Britain in that it is from a much older animal. The best meat is from bullocks of up to three years old, which are sturdy and of magnificent bearing.

When my mother cooks *ternera en salsa*, veal in sauce, and I tell her how delicious it is, she invariably replies, 'Well, it is perfectly plain.' This simplicity, however, is not so simply achieved. First she browns the meat well with a few small cloves of garlic, adding wine for a touch of drama and extra taste, then some good home-made veal stock if she has any or water if not. When the meat is tender and the sauce sufficiently concentrated, she usually adds some fresh peas and a few cubed potatoes, previously fried in olive oil. Alternatively she prepares veal with a stuffing of *tortillitas*, plain omelettes, York ham that she makes herself, and a few *manzanilla* olives cut into pieces. She insists, though, that one should always buy the olives with stones and remove them just before cooking. Another of my mother's favourite recipes is lamb *a la chilindrón*, made with fresh tomatoes and peppers.

One very traditional dish in Spain is the *cocido*, made with two or three kinds of meat – beef, chicken and pork in various forms. The pig is, indeed, the animal that has had the widest influence on the gastronomy of the country. It has been an important, and at times essential, part of the economy. In rural Spain, the *matanza*, or killing of the pig, used to represent happiness and the security of a full stomach.

Pork appears fresh; salted (*lacón*, for example); preserved in fat; as sausages that are made in a thousand different ways and places; and salt-cured to make the unrivalled hams that are produced everywhere. Hams from Jabugo in Huelva, Trevelez in Granada, Guijuelo in Salamanaca, Teruel, Catalonia and Valencia are the ones that spring most readily to mind.

The world of Spanish *embutidos*, or pork butchery, is so rich and colourful that every time I return from my homeland I bring back with me the memory of a new flavour, and a little more knowledge of a subject that I wonder if I will ever really know in full. In every corner of Spain, there is a culinary tradition in which pork products reign supreme, whether made from the Iberian pig, the handsome dark breed that roams free, or from the white European breeds. Blood sausages from Burgos, made with rice and pine kernels; tiny *chistorra* sausages from Pamplona, full of flavour and simply fried or served on skewers; white and black puddings (*botifarras*) from Catalonia with green and broad beans; a piece of *fuet* or *chorizo* with the bread of *la merienda*, the children's tea; or to accompany the *lacón con grelos* that so inspires me – the list is endless.

ROAST VENISON WITH APPLE
Venado Asado con Manzanas

A few years ago I was given a wonderful piece of venison. My friend Mari-Sol, who is an excellent home cook and lives in the lovely town of Aranjuez near Toledo, suggested I try this recipe. This dish can also be made with chestnuts instead of apples.

SERVES 4

For the marinade

500 ml (17 fl oz) red wine
50 ml (2 fl oz) olive oil
1 garlic clove, peeled and
  crushed
2 Spanish onions, peeled
  and finely chopped

2 glasses Spanish brandy
1 bay leaf
2 sprigs of thyme
6 black peppercorns, ground

1 kg (2 lb) prime venison
100 g (4 oz) butter
Salt and freshly ground
  black pepper
1 glass Spanish brandy

1 kg (2 lb) apples, peeled,
  cored and sliced
2 small Spanish onions,
  peeled and sliced

Mix all the marinade ingredients together in a large bowl and rub over the venison. Place the venison in the marinade, cover and leave for 2 days in a cool place, turning occasionally with wooden spoons.

Pre-heat the oven to 190°C/375°F/Gas 5. Remove the meat from the marinade, drain and dry it. Heat the butter in a flameproof casserole and fry the meat until browned on all sides. Season with salt and pepper, sprinkle with the brandy and surround with the apples and onions. Cover and cook for about 1½ hours until the meat is tender. Add a little cold water if the meat dries out during cooking.

When the meat is cooked, transfer it to a serving dish and keep warm. Purée the apples and onions, re-heat and serve as a sauce.

PORK WITH TURNIP TOPS
Lacón con Grelos

I enjoy the more complicated dishes of Galician cooking most during the winter, and none more so than this one which includes a delicious vegetable with a strong character of its own that is all too often overcooked: the *grelo* or turnip top. This is a dish made during carnival, and its star is the foreleg of the pig. It is served with a red Ribeiro wine drunk from little white porcelain cups that contrast with the almost purple colour of the young local wine.

I have much reduced the traditional cooking times for the potatoes and the greens, even though this is not exactly how the Galicians would do it. What I also do at home is to substitute a drizzle of olive oil for the pork fat, which is far more healthy, even though it may deprive the dish of a little of its charm.

SERVES 8

2.5 kg (5½ lb) hock of pork
10 potatoes, peeled
3 bunches turnip tops or
  spinach

8 small chorizo *sausages*
100 g (4 oz) pork fat, cubed
  or 4 tablespoons olive oil

Soak the pork in water for 24 hours to remove the salt, then drain and rinse.

Place the pork in a large saucepan and cover with water. Bring to the boil and simmer for 3 hours, then transfer the pork to a serving dish. Use the water to boil the potatoes, turnip tops, *chorizos* and pork fat or olive oil for about 20–30 minutes until tender. Serve the vegetables and pork piping hot.

PORK FILLET WITH ALMONDS
Lomo de Cerdo Almendrado

This recipe belongs to a friend, Inés, in Cádiz. The addition of cream is a result of the French heritage in the cooking of Jerez. It is a wonderfully simple recipe, but very tasty with the delicious almond stuffing and cream sauce.

SERVES 4

1 kg (2 lb) pork fillet
100 g (4 oz) almonds,
    toasted and skinned
1 tablespoon plain flour
Salt and freshly ground
    black pepper
2 tablespoons olive oil

1 glass dry sherry
1 Spanish onion, peeled and
    chopped
300 ml (10 fl oz) chicken
    stock
150 ml (5 fl oz) cream

Open out the fillet without cutting right through it. Crush the almonds and place them in the centre of the meat. Fold it together and tie it neatly. Dust the meat with flour and season to taste with salt and pepper. Heat the oil and fry the meat until browned, then add the sherry and simmer for 5 minutes. Finally, add the onion and fry until soft. Pour in the stock and bring to the boil. Cover and simmer until the meat is tender. Remove the meat from the pan. Cut it into slices and arrange on a warmed serving plate. Stir the cream into the sauce, re-heat and pour over the meat.

MEATBALLS
Albóndigas

This is one of the dishes I call 'school food', although it is one I always liked. When we make meatballs at home we simply add some bread that has been soaked in water and drained, a whole egg, parsley and chopped garlic to make the meat, which should be very lean, succulent and tasty. Every household has its own formula: although the results may be similar, the cook always imparts his or her own personality.

SERVES 4

1 kg (2 lb) lean minced beef
2 eggs
2 tablespoons fresh breadcrumbs
3 garlic cloves, peeled and crushed
1 tablespoon chopped fresh parsley
500 g (1 lb 2 oz) Spanish onions, peeled and chopped

Salt and freshly ground black pepper
1 tablespoon plain flour
3 tablespoons olive oil
2 small tomatoes, skinned, do seeded and chopped
1 small glass dry white wine
150 ml (5 fl oz) chicken stock

Mix the meat, eggs, breadcrumbs, garlic, parsley and half the onions, and season with a little salt and pepper. Form into small balls and dust with flour. Heat the oil in a flameproof casserole and sauté the meatballs until well browned on all sides. Add the remaining onion to the pan and cook until soft. Add the tomatoes, wine and stock. Season to taste with salt and pepper. Cover and simmer for 45 minutes.

VEAL WITH WILD MUSHROOMS
Fricandó con Setas

This *fricandó* has little to do with the French dish from which it originally derived. In Catalonia, the *Moixerdon* mushrooms, specially dried for the preparation of this recipe, are the favoured ones, though any other fresh or dried mushrooms will do. Of the many versions I have tasted in Barcelona, this is the one I like best. The meat should be beautifully tender, covered in a creamy smooth sauce.

SERVES 4

500 g (1 lb 2 oz) wild
    mushrooms, dried or fresh
    (soaked weight)
1 kg (2 lb) piece of veal or
    beef, cut into small
    scallops
Salt
50 g (2 oz) plain flour
300 ml (10 fl oz) olive oil
2 Spanish onions, peeled
    and sliced
2 carrots, sliced
6 ripe tomatoes, skinned,
    de-seeded and chopped

2 glasses dry white wine
150 ml (5 fl oz) meat stock
    or water
1 bay leaf
1 sprig of thyme
1 sprig of oregano
Freshly ground black pepper
2 garlic cloves, peeled and
    chopped
25 g (1 oz) almonds,
    toasted, skinned and
    crushed

If you are using dried mushrooms, soak them in water for 2 hours, then drain.

Season the meat with a little salt and coat with flour. Heat a little oil in a frying-pan and brown the meat, then transfer it to a flameproof earthenware casserole. Heat 200 ml (7 fl oz) of oil and sauté the onions and carrots for a few minutes until they begin to soften, then add the tomatoes and fry for 3 minutes. Pour in the wine. Bring to the boil and simmer until the liquid has reduced slightly. Pour the sauce over the meat in the casserole and add enough stock or water just to cover the meat. Tie the bay leaf, thyme and oregano together to make a bouquet garni and add it to the dish. Cover and simmer gently for about 30 minutes until the meat is tender. Remove the lid and continue to simmer for a further 10 minutes until the liquid has reduced. Remove the meat from the casserole, strain the sauce if you wish, then return the meat and vegetables to the casserole. Season to taste with salt and pepper.

Meanwhile, heat the remaining oil and sauté the mushrooms with the garlic for 3 minutes then add them to the casserole with the almonds. Cook for a few minutes and remove the bouquet garni before serving.

VEAL WITH ORANGE AND WINE
Ternera a la Naranja y al Vino

This is my recipe developed from some notes I jotted down in Valencia, and I have been cooking it for more years than I care to admit. It is the sort of dish that always turns out well, as long as it is made for no more than 4 people. Once the meat has been rolled up and secured with cocktail sticks or string, the most important thing is to fry the meat rolls very quickly so that they colour well but stay rare inside. The orange colour of the sauce makes it very appetizing and attractive; a light but rich-tasting dish.

SERVES 4

4 large slices York ham
8 small veal escalopes
Salt and freshly ground
black pepper
2 tablespoons olive oil

2 small Spanish onions or
shallots, peeled and
chopped
1 glass Amontillado sherry
300 ml (10 fl oz) orange
juice

For the garnish

1 orange, sliced   *1 bunch of watercress*

Place half a slice of ham inside each escalope, roll them up and secure with cocktail sticks. Season to taste with salt and pepper. Heat the oil and fry the onions or shallots until transparent. Add the rolls of meat and fry quickly over a high heat until golden-brown. Pour in the sherry, bring to the boil, and boil until the liquid has reduced by half. Add the orange juice, cover and simmer gently for about 30 minutes until the meat is tender. Transfer the escalopes to a warmed serving dish and keep them warm. Boil the sauce for a few minutes until it has reduced and thickened slightly, then pour over the meat and serve garnished with orange slices and watercress.

OXTAIL
Rabo de Toro

Every time I visit Córdoba, one of the most beautiful cities in Spain, I stop at the El Caballo Rojo restaurant situated in the city centre near to La Mezquita. Here they serve *El Rabo de*

Toro, oxtail, which is without doubt one of the tastiest dishes which I recommend to all my friends. Serve it with a *panaché*, or arrangement, of boiled courgettes and carrots.

SERVES 4

200 ml (7 fl oz) olive oil
2 garlic cloves, peeled and
    sliced
4 Spanish onions, peeled
    and cut into julienne
    strips
16 small onions, peeled
1/2 stick celery, cut into
    julienne strips
4 carrots, cut into julienne
    strips
A few black peppercorns
1 sprig of thyme
1 bay leaf
1 sprig of parsley
1.5 kg (3 lb) oxtail, cut into
    pieces
Salt and freshly ground
    black pepper
50 g (2 oz) plain flour
1 glass dry wine, preferably
    Montilla
6 ripe tomatoes, skinned,
    de-seeded and chopped
100 ml (3 1/2 fl oz) veal or
    chicken stock

Heat most of the oil in a large flameproof casserole and fry the garlic until it begins to brown. Add the onions, celery, carrots, peppercorns, thyme, bay leaf and parsley. Fry gently until the onions are brown. Season the oxtail with salt and pepper, and dust with flour. Heat a little oil in a second pan and fry the meat until just browned. Transfer the meat on to the vegetable base in the casserole. Add the wine and tomatoes, cover and simmer for 10 minutes. Pour in the stock, cover and simmer gently for 2 hours, adding a drop more stock if the stew begins to dry out.

When the oxtail is tender, remove it from the casserole and strain the sauce if you prefer it thin. Return the oxtail and sauce to the casserole and simmer for 5 minutes before serving very hot.

FILLET STEAK ON A BED OF SWEET AND SOUR ONIONS
Solomillo al Agridulce de Cebolla

I think the first time I had fillet steak must have been outside Spain because this cut of meat had always been way beyond my mother's food budget. This is a recipe that combines onion, which is such an essential part of Spanish cookery, with the sweet and sour flavours we have inherited from our Moorish forebears. The meat cooks beautifully: browned on the outside and rare and succulent inside.

SERVES 4

400 g (14 oz) Spanish
   onions, peeled and cut
   into julienne strips
100 g (4 oz) butter
2 tablespoons sherry vinegar
800 g (1¾ lb) fillet steak,
   cut into 4

Salt and freshly ground
   black pepper
4 tablespoons honey
4 tablespoons meat stock
1 sprig of mint to garnish

Pre-heat the oven to 180°C/350°F/Gas 4.

Place the onions in a roasting tin with a little butter and bake for 15 minutes. Stir in 1 tablespoon of sherry vinegar and bake for a further 10–15 minutes until the onions are white and almost transparent.

Meanwhile, melt the remaining butter in a large pan, season the meat with salt and pepper and lightly fry until it is browned, being careful not to allow the butter to burn. Drain off some of the fat and and pour in the rest of the sherry vinegar, stirring to deglaze the pan. Add the honey and boil to reduce the sauce slightly, then add the stock and boil until the sauce has reduced to the consistency you prefer, turning the meat occasionally. Check and adjust the seasoning if necessary, and add a little more honey or sherry vinegar if the sauce is too sweet or too sour.

Arrange the onions on a warmed serving plate, set the meat on top and cover with the sauce. Garnish with the mint and serve immediately.

MADRILIAN-STYLE STEW
Cocido Madrileño

My mother, who is not from Madrid, used to make this incredible combination of dishes on Mondays, the day she did the washing. The soup, the chick peas and the vegetables were always just as highly praised as the meat, the black pudding and the exquisite tomato sauce she made. Later on, my father gave her a pressure cooker as a present for which, good cook as she was, she had no desire. Still, Monday's life in the Sevilla household changed, if only because she no longer had to worry about watching the pot all morning long. Her *cocido*, however, did not change, and continued to be as good as ever. Spanish black puddings are the best to use, but you can use whatever type is available. Serve the soup, followed by the 2 plates of meat and vegetables with a fresh Tomato Sauce (see page 109).

SERVES 4–6

500 g (1 lb 2 oz) chick peas
1 salty pig's trotter
200 g (7 oz) stewing beef
1/2 corn-fed chicken
100 g (4 oz) piece of
    Serrano ham or dry-cured
    ham
100 g (4 oz) pork fat
1/2 small Spanish onion,
    peeled
6 cloves

1 kg (2 lb) seasonal
    vegetables (cabbage,
    green beans or spinach)
2 small Spanish black
    puddings
2 chorizo sausages
6 small potatoes, peeled
100 g (4 oz) soup pasta
50 ml (2 fl oz) olive oil
1 garlic clove, peeled and
    chopped
Salt

Soak the chick peas and pig's trotter separately overnight in cold water. Drain and rinse.

Place the meat, chicken, ham and fat in a large pan, cover with cold water and bring to the boil. Add the chick peas and the pig's trotter. Pierce the onion with the cloves and add it to the pan. Bring back to the boil, cover and simmer for 3 hours.

Place the vegetables, black puddings and *chorizos* in a second pan and just cover with salted water. Bring to the boil, cover and simmer for about 10 minutes, then add the potatoes and cook for a further 15–20 minutes.

To prepare the soup, strain the stock from the meat and chick peas into a clean pan, add the pasta and simmer for 10 minutes until cooked. Cut the meat into pieces. Place the chick peas on a warmed serving plate and arrange the meat on top, with the ham, pig's trotter, chicken and bacon fat around it. Heat the oil in a separate pan and fry the garlic until just browned. Strain the vegetables, dress with the oil and garlic and arrange on a serving plate with the potatoes, sliced *chorizo* and black pudding.

SPIT-ROAST KIDNEYS
Riñones Ensartados

This is a perfect starter, especially if you thread the kidneys on to little wooden skewers.

SERVES 4

6 small lambs' kidneys, skinned and cored

Salt

1 garlic clove, peeled and quartered

1 tablespoon white wine vinegar

8 rashers bacon, rinded and cut into pieces

2 corn-fed chicken breasts, thinly sliced

100 g (4 oz) ham, sliced

150 g (5 oz) fresh breadcrumbs

Freshly ground black pepper

2 eggs, beaten

250 ml (8 fl oz) olive oil

1 bunch of watercress

Soak the kidneys for 3 hours in salted water with the garlic and wine vinegar. Meanwhile, soak some small wooden kebab skewers in water. Rinse the kidneys in warm water, then in several changes of cold water. Slice the kidneys thinly, then thread them on to the skewers, alternating kidney, bacon, chicken and ham until the skewers are almost full. Sprinkle lightly with breadcrumbs and season to taste with pepper. Dip the kebabs in the egg and coat in bread crumbs, then dip in egg and breadcrumbs again. Heat the oil until very hot and fry the kebabs for about 10 minutes until golden-brown on all sides. Season the watercress well with salt and pepper and arrange it on a serving plate. Top with the kebabs and serve.

CASTILIAN ROAST LAMB
Cordero Asado Castellano

Traditionally, in Old and New Castile, the meat of very young lambs has been roasted in wood-fired ovens at a very high temperature, becoming crispy and always mouthwatering. The roasting of lambs born around Christmas time is very popular as the main dish during the festivities. I sometimes go to visit friends in Wales, and if I am there at the time of year when the farmers sell baby lambs, I buy enough to cook this recipe, or I adapt it slightly to my own requirements.

SERVES 6–8

1 sprig of tarragon
1 sprig of marjoram
1 glass dry white wine, preferably from La Mancha
1 × 2 kg (4½ lb) double best end of lamb (14–16 ribs)
100 ml (4 fl oz) olive oil

Salt
1 small bay leaf
150 g (5 oz) Spanish onions, peeled and diced
3 garlic cloves, peeled and crushed
1 teaspoon paprika
500 g (1 lb 2 oz) small roasting potatoes, peeled

Place the tarragon and marjoram in the wine and leave to macerate for a few hours.

Have your butcher prepare your double best end of lamb. If you wish to do it yourself, first cut either side of the backbone with a meat saw to free the rib bones, taking care not to cut all the way through to the back flesh and skin, and keeping both sides intact. With the point of a sharp knife, gently cut the meat from each vertebra to free the backbone.

188

Trim the meat from the tip of each rib bone to form a cutlet end. To tie and shape, lay the joint on its side like a book, place the string around the middle from end to end, tie a slip knot to hold, then stand the joint on its back and tighten the string to pull both sides together to form a cup shape cavity to hold the *aderezo*, or dressing. Insert the backbone inside the cavity and transfer the joint to an oiled roasting dish. Lightly brush the skin with olive oil and sprinkle with salt.

Pre-heat the oven to 200°C/400°F/Gas 6. To make the *aderezo*, combine the bay leaf, onions, garlic, paprika, remaining olive oil and salt to taste, then pour in the wine and herbs. Spoon the *aderezo* into the cavity of the lamb, surround the joint with the potatoes and roast for 35 minutes. Brush the potatoes with the fat in the dish, reduce the heat to 180°C/350°F/Gas 4 and continue cooking for a further 30–40 minutes or until the meat is cooked to your liking and the potatoes are golden-brown and tender. Remove the string and backbone. Carve and serve.

RIOJAN LAMB STEW
Caldereta de Cordero a la Riojana

This lamb stew is one of the specialities of the itinerant herdsmen and is full of the produce of the fertile Riojan valleys, including tiny, tender artichokes. I recommend drinking a glass or two of a good Rioja Reserva with it.

SERVES 4

300 ml (10 fl oz) olive oil
1 kg (2 lb) shoulder of lamb,
  boned and cubed
1 Spanish onion, peeled and
  finely chopped
2 carrots, peeled and
  chopped
1 leek, chopped
Salt
1½ tablespoons plain flour
2 tomatoes, skinned, de-
  seeded and puréed

1 garlic clove, peeled
1 sprig of parsley, chopped
4 tablespoons chicken stock
  or water
3 small globe artichokes,
  trimmed and quartered
2 tablespoons lemon juice
250 g (9 oz) shelled peas
250 g (9 oz) potatoes, peeled
  and diced

Heat 250 ml (8 fl oz) of oil in a flameproof casserole and fry the meat until browned. Add the onion, carrots and leek, season with salt and fry until golden-brown. Stir in the flour and tomatoes. Use a mortar and pestle to pound the garlic and parsley or finely chop them together using a knife, then add the stock or water to make a paste. Stir this into the pan.

Meanwhile, cook the artichokes in boiling salted water with the lemon juice for about 10 minutes until tender, then drain them and add them to the pan with the peas. Add a little more water or stock, if necessary. Lower the heat, cover and simmer gently for about 20 minutes until everything is cooked, stirring occasionally.

Heat the remaining oil and fry the potatoes until golden-brown. Add them to the pan just before serving.

DESSERTS
AND SWEETS
Postres y Dulces

My grandfather, like my father, had a very sweet tooth. On Sundays, he had the happy habit of buying a tray of pastries on his way home from church. For me, Sunday lunches seemed to last for ever, especially since my brother always ate very slowly. Having finally brought in the parcel, still wrapped up in the local pastry-shop paper, my mother would cut the silk ribbon somewhat ceremoniously and slowly show us the contents. Even then, the waiting was not over. Since I was the youngest, and a girl, I was the last to choose from the tray full of fine pastries. Small cream-filled profiteroles (my favourites, which I still make with caramel); little mille-feuilles filled with *cabello de angel*, threads of sweet pumpkin; tiny éclairs filled with chocolate or mocha-flavoured confectioner's custard; little baskets of fruit . . . endless delights and temptations.

The Spanish custom of bringing a dessert, as my grandfather did on Sundays, is a way of thanking the person who has invited one to share their table: on the whole, we Spaniards are not great makers of puddings at home. Fresh fruit has always been the classic dessert in Spain. The winter brings oranges and mandarins, as well as pears and the little

Canary Island bananas. One day, though, one would come home from school and find small bowls for washing fruit set out on a tray in the kitchen: summer had arrived! Henceforth, dessert would be a celebration every day: plums, deep red picota cherries, Claudia plums, sweet apricots and peaches, Piel de Sapo melons and sweet, red water melons.

It was a rare event for my father to make crème caramels, *natillas* (egg custard) or rice pudding which was his true speciality. My mother, too, preferred to apply her culinary skills to other kinds of recipes, except for birthday cakes, *torrijas* (bread and milk fries) for Holy Week, and occasional apple and caramel tarts or *rosquillas*, little fried pastries.

If this regimen applied in my house, it did and still does apply in the majority of restaurants across the country. You will find that the dessert menu is limited to one or two local specialties, plus fruit, ice-cream, cheese and crème caramel. Having said that, however, things have changed slightly over the last ten years. The new tendencies that have emerged at the hands of professionals, fired by a sense of adventure, have refined and lightened many of the traditional puddings, as well as creating new ones that can easily stand competition against anything on my grandfather's tray.

It is the regional specialities that I most enjoy and would recommend, as long as they have been made according to the spirit, if not the letter, of the artisan's tradition. Let me take you through some of the most familiar and delicious.

To eat *filloas*, delicious thin lace pancakes, in a restaurant in Madrid or Barcelona is always a treat. Even so, my memory takes me back most readily to a fiesta in Muros in La Coruña in the middle of August, when the whole of Galicia goes on a *romería*, and thoroughly enjoys itself. It was pouring with rain and, under a huge umbrella and at great speed, a village woman was making delicate *filloas* in two *filloerías*, or frying-pans, set on hot coals. Three or four children were also huddled under the umbrella, pesetas clutched in somewhat damp hands, patiently waiting their turn to buy.

The milk-based puddings still made by the shepherds in the Basque Country and the Catalan Pyrenees bring back other delicious memories. Properly made, these set milk puddings, *mamía* and *recuit*, are a far cary from what is served in coastal and city restaurants under the same names.

Although the Spaniards are not that keen on desserts, Spain does have an extensive culture and tradition of making and eating sweets. Some extremely sweet ones we owe partly to the Moors and Christians, and partly to the Jews. The Moors taught us to use almonds and honey to make *turrón*, a delicious confection, and also introduced marzipan. From the Christian convents, we inherited a whole culture of excellent recipes which have come down to us today almost unchanged. If you ever go through Toledo, Valencia or Seville – the three most important cities in the realm of Spanish confectionery – do try the sweets on offer there, expecially the figures and fruits made of marzipan.

Other sweets, biscuits and pastries are traditionally associated with religious festivals. *Arnadi* is a dessert made during Holy Week in the Spanish Levante. Of unquestionable Moorish origin, it consists of the flesh of roasted pumpkin, scraped out and baked in an earthenware container until caramelized. Served covered with currants, pine kernels and almonds, it is a bit cloying for me although I find the flavour and texture interesting. Another famous sweet which is still served in bars and sold in pastry shops is the *pestiño*. This is a sweet fritter made from an elastic dough of flour, oil, red and white wine, salt and sesame seed. The nuns in Seville bake them in a honey and sugar syrup, then roll them in sesame seeds. One thing I do absolutely crave is *flao*. This baked confection is filled with a fresh, soft cream cheese made from ewes' milk, with cinnamon, sugar, egg and a little ground almond, and covered with *pa-noli*, a kind of pastry made from flour, oil and *aguardiente* (*eau-de-vie*). If you ever come across *flaos*, be sure to try one . . . or two.

QUINCE PASTE
Dulce de Membrillo

I do not consider this to be a dessert in the strict sense of the word. Rather I have always used it as a good alternative to chocolate, ham and the preserved meats that are served with bread as the standard tea-time fare put together by children all over Spain when they get home from school at about six in the evening. *Membrillo* is also served for breakfast with a good Manchego, Roncal or Idiazábal cheese.

SERVES 4

1.5 kg (3 lb) yellow quinces   250 ml (8 fl oz) water
450 g (1 lb) sugar

Rub the quinces clean and place in a saucepan of cold water. Heat until the skins look as if they are about to split, then remove them from the water, skin them and discard the pips and membranes.

Dissolve the sugar in the water and heat gently to make a syrup. Add the fruit to the syrup, making sure that there is enough syrup to cover the fruit. Leave to cool.

WALNUT CREAM
Intzaursalsa

This a very old recipe from the *caserío*, or Basque farmhouse, where there are always one or two walnut trees which give an excellent crop each year. Today, the new Basque cooking uses this recipe as a part of its novel confections with excellent results, combining it with all sorts of flavours and textures, but I still prefer it the way it is made by María Dolores, the cook at the little hotel in Errazu, in the Pyrenees. Here is her recipe.

SERVES 4

200 g (7 oz) shelled walnuts
750 ml (1¼ pints) water
1 stick cinnamon
750 ml (1¼ pints) milk

200 g (7 oz) sugar
1 teaspoon ground
   cinnamon

Wrap the walnuts in a thick white cloth and crush them with a mallet until they form a thick paste. This is the traditional method, but you can grind them to a paste in a food processor if you prefer. Bring the water to the boil with the cinnamon and add the walnut paste. Leave to simmer for about 12 minutes until the liquid has almost evaporated, then remove the cinnamon stick and add the milk and sugar. Simmer for about 30 minutes until the mixture thickens to form a light cream. Serve warm in individual dishes sprinkled with ground cinnamon.

ⓥ CHRISTMAS EVE FRUIT STEW
Compota de Nochebuena

This is very similar to the *compota* made by my Navarrese grandmother, and is one of the dishes that has always been prepared in my family on special days, religious or not. The difference is that she would add a drop of wine, whereas I prefer the gentler taste of my adaptation. In the winter in Spain, we make *compotas* containing nuts and dried fruit, but I also love the summer ones using seasonal fruit, including berries from trees or from bushes, especially gooseberries.

SERVES 4

50 g (2 oz) dried figs
100 g (4 oz) prunes
100 g (4 oz) dried apricots
50 g (2 oz) stoned dates
50 g (2 oz) currants
100 g (4 oz) peeled
  chestnuts
A few aniseed seeds
1 vanilla pod

100 g (4 oz) sugar
150 ml (5 fl oz) water
Grated rind of ½ orange
½ stick cinnamon
1 pear, peeled, cored and
  sliced
1 red-skinned apple, peeled,
  cored and sliced

Soak all the dried fruits in water for 12 hours, then drain and rinse.

Place the chestnuts in a saucepan with the aniseed seeds and vanilla pod. Just cover with water and bring to the boil. Cover the pan and simmer for 20 minutes until the chestnuts are tender. Drain and remove the vanilla pod.

Dissolve the sugar in the water with the orange rind, cinnamon and vanilla pod. Simmer for 5 minutes to make a syrup. Add the soaked fruit to the syrup in the order listed in the ingredients, adding the chestnuts after the dates, then add the pear and apple. Stir well and cook for a further 5 minutes. Leave to cool before serving.

ⓥ SUGAR-COATED FRIED BREAD
Torrijas

I used to dread Holy Week as a child, because I was made to stay silent for hours on end every day, but I was always cheered up by the *torrijas* that were made for dessert or tea. They can sometimes be found at other times of the year in a few of Madrid's cafés where they are always delicious. People still make them at home, using all kinds of bread, even the sweet Swiss bread, but the best are made from the long French-style loaves cut into slices about 2.5 cm (1 in) thick.

SERVES 4-6

600 ml (1 pint) milk
1 small stick cinnamon
100 g (4 oz) sugar
1 French loaf, cut into thick
* slices*
2 eggs, beaten
100 ml (3½ fl oz) olive oil
1 tablespoon caster sugar
1 teaspoon ground
* cinnamon*

Bring the milk, cinnamon stick and sugar to the boil. Discard the cinnamon stick, and pour the milk over the bread slices, making sure they are thoroughly soaked. Dip the bread slices in beaten egg. Heat the oil and fry the bread until golden-brown on both sides, then drain on a wire rack. Mix the caster sugar and cinnamon and roll the *torrijas* in the spiced sugar before serving.

Ⓥ

PUFFS OF AIR
Buñuelos de Viento

Although the recipe for these puffs is from Madrid, the special *buñuelo* shops in the Barceloneta area of Barcelona make ones that are particularly light. I love to sit on a bench in the spring sunshine in this Mediterranean port, eating hollow *buñuelos*, sprinkled with lots of sugar, out of a paper cone. The cone keeps them warm until they are gone and, needless to say, they disappear – like all good things – far to fast. Some traditional recipes make the *buñuelos* with yeast, but I find this choux pastry very effective.

SERVES 4

For the dough

5 tablespoons milk
5 tablespoons water
25 g (1 oz) butter
A pinch of salt
25 g (1 oz) caster sugar
1 tablespoon Spanish
    brandy

Grated rind of 1 lemon
50 g (2 oz) plain flour
2 eggs, beaten
1 egg white

For the filling

2 eggs
75 g (3 oz) caster sugar
75 g (3 oz) plain flour

500 ml (17 fl oz) milk
Grated rind of 1 lemon
25 g (1 oz) butter

250 ml (8 fl oz) olive oil
2 tablespoons icing sugar

1 teaspoon ground
    cinnamon

Pour the milk and water into a saucepan with the butter, salt, sugar, brandy and lemon rind. Heat gently until the butter melts, then bring quickly to the boil. Remove from the heat and pour in the flour all at once. Beat with a wooden spoon until the dough comes away cleanly from the sides of the pan. Place the dough in a mixing bowl and put to one side to cool a little. Then blend in the eggs and egg white, a little at a time.

To make the filling, mix the eggs and sugar in a bowl. Add the flour and a little cold milk to loosen the mixture. Bring the remaining milk to the boil in a saucepan with the lemon rind. Add the egg mixture and cook over a low heat, stirring continuously with a wooden spoon, for 5 minutes. Remove from the heat and blend in the butter. Cover with greaseproof paper and leave to cool.

Heat the oil in a deep frying-pan. Roll small pieces of the dough, about the size of a small walnut, between 2 spoons and fry them in the hot oil. Do not fry too many puffs at once as they can stick together. When the puffs have doubled in size and turned over, push them towards the centre of the pan so that they cook until golden-brown. Remove from the pan, drain and leave to dry, but keep them warm. Once dry, cut them on one side with a pair of scissors ready to fill with the filling.

Place the filling in a piping bag and fill each puff. Serve hot, sprinkled with icing sugar and cinnamon.

MAMÍA AND APPLE PASTRIES
Hojaldre de Mamía con Manzana Reineta

This is a deliciously light puff pastry slice filled with apples lightly flavoured with lemon and apple liqueur. Instead of a cream filling, we use this natural junket or *mamía*, which in Spain is made with ewes' milk. If you like making puff pastry you can, of course, use your own recipe, but frozen pastry gives excellent results in much less time. For the decoration, you can use any attractively coloured fruit with a fairly strong flavour to complement the pastry. A sweet but very light wine such as Mistela Argía, which is made in the Basque Country, is an ideal accompaniment.

SERVES 4

250 g (9 oz) puff pastry
2 tablespoons icing sugar
600 ml (1 pint) milk
1 teaspoon rennet essence
10 g (¼ oz) gelatine
4 tablespoons water
3 tablespoons sugar

4 small Reineta or cooking apples, peeled and cored
Grated rind of ½ small lemon
1 tablespoon Sagardoz or apple liqueur
100 g (4 oz) strawberries or raspberries

Pre-heat the oven to 230°C/450°F/Gas 8.

Roll out the pastry until it is about 5 mm (¼ in) thick, then cut it into long thin triangles measuring about 15 × 15 × 7.5 cm (6 × 6 × 3 inch). Place on a damp baking sheet and bake for about 8 minutes. Just before the pastry is ready, remove it from the oven and dust with icing sugar. Return it to the oven for a further 3–4 minutes until the pastry is well risen and the sugar has caramelized.

Remove from the oven and leave to cool. Split the pastry in half horizontally.

Warm the milk to blood heat, add the rennet and stir for a few seconds. Leave the rennet at room temperature for 15 minutes to set. Dissolve the gelatine in 2 tablespoons of water with 1 tablespoon of sugar. Warm the mixture over a bowl of hot water to make sure that the gelatine has fully dissolved. Whisk this gently into the *mamía* and allow it to cool and set.

Place the apples in a saucepan with the remaining water and sugar, the lemon rind and *Sagardoz* or apple liqueur. Poach gently for about 10 minutes, basting occasionally with the syrup, until the apples are cooked. Remove from the heat, slice thinly and leave to cool.

When ready to serve, spoon a layer of *mamía* over the pastry bases, without stirring the *mamía*. Top with sliced apple, then with the top layer of pastry. Decorate with the strawberries or raspberries and serve immediately.

Ⓥ

LACE PANCAKES
FROM GALICIA
Fillous

The word *filloa* comes from the Latin *folio*, meaning leaf. They are quite unlike other delicious versions, such as the French crêpe, although, in the same way as these, you can serve both sweet ones for dessert and savoury ones as a first course. My favourite savoury fillings are cheese and spinach, or a sauce of onions, tomatoes and tinned tuna.

Originally they were made on huge circular stones which were heated in a fire before the *filloa* paste was spread on them. I prepare mine in a food processor and fry them in a cast-iron pan.

MAKES 8 PANCAKES

100 g (4 oz) plain flour   *500 ml (17 fl oz) milk*
Salt   *5 eggs, well beaten*
250 ml (8 fl oz) water

Put the flour and a little salt in a bowl and gradually blend in the water and milk. Then mix in the eggs and beat well. Rest the mixture in the refrigerator for a couple of hours before using.

Heat the pan. Pour in a spoonful of batter, at the same time brushing it across the pan. Use as little batter as possible so that the pancakes are really thin. Cook one side, then carefully turn the pancake using a palette knife and cook the other side. Remove from the pan and keep the pancakes warm while you continue to fry the remaining batter.

ⓋSPONGE CAKES WITH OLIVE OIL
Magdalenas

These are small light cakes ideal for tea-time, with a subtle lemon taste. They show that you can use olive oil for any recipe, as we do in Spain.

SERVES 4

225 g (8 oz) plain flour   *200 ml (7 fl oz) olive oil*
100 g (4 oz) caster sugar   *6 eggs, separated*
Grated rind of 1 lemon   *2 tablespoons milk*

Pre-heat the oven to 190°C/375°F/Gas 5.

Mix the flour, sugar and lemon rind, then add the oil, egg

yolks and milk, and mix until smooth. Whisk the egg whites until stiff, then fold them into the mixture. Spoon the mixture into well-greased deep bun tins and bake in the oven for 20 minutes.

Ⓥ CANARY CHEESE TARTS
Quesadillas de Hierro

The first time I tried this dessert was in a little restaurant in that part of the island of Santa Cruz de Tenerife called Gigante. The cook had been born on Hierro, another of the Canary Islands and the birthplace of this recipe which she would make for afternoon tea.

SERVES 4

50 g (2 oz) butter
50 g (2 oz) caster sugar
1 egg yolk
225 g (8 oz) soft Hierro or curd cheese
50 g (2 oz) flaked almonds

Grated rind and juice of ½ lemon
2 egg whites
225 g (8 oz) shortcrust pastry
1 egg, beaten

Pre-heat the oven to 180°C/350°F/Gas 4.

Cream the butter and sugar until light and fluffy, then gradually beat in the egg yolk. Add the cheese, almonds and lemon rind and juice. Whisk the egg whites until they form stiff peaks and fold them into the mixture.

Roll out the pastry and use it to line lightly greased tart tins, fluting the edges with your fingers. Fill with the cheese mixture. Brush the edges of the pastry with beaten egg and bake for 20 minutes until the filling is firm and golden-brown.

Ⓥ ALMOND AND CINNAMON SWEETS
Alfajores

There are many versions of this kind of sweet and the size can vary from one convent or pastry shop to another.

SERVES 4

500 g (1 lb 2 oz) almonds, skinned

500 g (1 lb 2 oz) granulated sugar

120 ml (4 fl oz) water

A pinch of ground cinnamon

Grated rind of ½ lemon

Rice paper wafers

Soak the almonds in cold water overnight until soft, then drain and pound or process to a paste.

Put the sugar and water in a heavy-based pan, bring to the boil and boil, without stirring, until the syrup turns pale golden and can be pulled into thin strands. Keep the mixture over a low heat and mix in the almonds to form a paste. Then add the cinnamon and lemon rind. Remove from the heat and work the paste with a wooden spoon until it is well mixed and has cooled slightly. Place spoonfuls on to the rice wafers and cover each one with another wafer.

Ⓥ SEVENTH HEAVEN WITH RASPBERRY SAUCE
Tocinillo de Cielo con Salsa de Frambuesa

This recipe is from José María, master *pâtissier* at La Esperanza, one of the best pastry shops in Jerez de la Frontera.

I recommend you make it in tiny timbales because it is extremely sweet. The raspberry sauce contributes a touch of acidity, which means you can eat a little more.

SERVES 4–6

For the raspberry sauce
200 g (7 oz) raspberries   *50 g (2 oz) caster sugar*

For the caramel
225 g (8 oz) caster sugar   *150 ml (5 fl oz) water*

For the tocinillo
275 g (10 oz) caster sugar   *10 egg yolks, beaten*
120 ml (4 fl oz) water

To make the sauce, mix the raspberries and sugar and leave to macerate for 2 hours, stirring occasionally. Then rub this through a sieve.

To make the caramel, dissolve the sugar in the water completely in a small saucepan. Then boil until it takes on a golden colour. Remove from the heat and pour into individual timbales or small moulds.

To prepare the syrup for the *tocinillos*, dissolve the sugar in the water. Then bring to the boil until the right consistency is achieved at a heat of 113–115°C (236–240°F).

Gently break the egg yolks in a bowl and, once the syrup has cooled down a little, pour it very slowly into the egg yolks, mixing constantly with a wooden spoon. Strain and pour the egg mixture into the timbales. Place them in a steamer and cook for a few minutes until they set.

Before turning them out on to individual plates make certain they have cooled down properly. Surround with raspberry sauce.

Ⓥ

NOUGAT
Turrón de Alicante y de Jijona

In all the twenty years I have lived in Britain we have spent every Christmas in Madrid with my family. The children, who are not children any longer, still prepare the Christmas sweet tray at the beginning of the afternoon on Christmas Eve. First, they cut up the 7 or 8 different kinds of *turrón*: Alicante (the hard one), Jijona (the soft one), chocolate, egg yolk, dark *guirlache*, fig paste and so on. Next, they set out the crystallized fruit, the marzipan figurines and, lastly, the plain and sugared pine nuts, and almonds, *peladillas*. During the next couple of days, they replace the sweets as they disappear, which is not just when it is time for dessert.

SERVES 24

For the Alicante style

Rice paper wafers
175 g (6 oz) honey
1½ tablespoons water
100 g (4 oz) caster sugar

1 egg white
350 g (12 oz) almonds, skinned and split
Grated rind of ½ lemon

For the Jijona style

Rice paper wafers
150 g (5 oz) almonds, skinned
150 g (5 oz) hazelnuts

3 egg whites
150 g (5 oz) caster sugar
150 g (5 oz) white honey
1 teaspoon cinnamon

For the Alicante style, line some bun tins with rice paper and have some circles of rice paper ready to place on the top. Heat the honey and water gently in a heavy-based pan until all the water has evaporated, then stir in the sugar with a wooden spoon. Whisk the egg white until it forms stiff peaks, then fold it into the honey and sugar. Stir gently over a low heat until the mixture turns to caramel, then immediately add the almonds and lemon rind and mix well. Pour the almond mixture quickly into the prepared tins, cover with another rice paper wafer and a baking sheet and weigh down until set.

For the Jijona style, have the bun tins prepared in the same way. Roast the skinned almonds under the grill for a few minutes until they begin to brown. Dry roast the hazelnuts in a pan for a few minutes until the skins are dry and the nuts begin to colour. Rub off the skins by rolling the nuts about in a clean cloth. Use a mortar and pestle or food processor to grind the roasted nuts finely. Whisk the egg whites until they form stiff peaks and fold in the ground nuts. Bring the sugar and honey to the boil in a heavy-based pan, then add the nut and egg white mixture and cook over a low heat for 10 minutes, stirring constantly with a spatula. Remove the mixture from the heat, turn into the prepared tins and cover with rice paper. When cold, remove the paper and sprinkle with cinnamon.

ⓋWALNUT CAKE
Pastel de Nueces

One of the gastronomic legacies of the Moorish occupation is the Spanish predilection for all kinds of nuts, which they use in a large variety of desserts and cakes. Nina is originally from Rioja, but she now owns a marvellous restaurant in the harbour area of Castellón de la Plana in Valencia. She makes a whole range of sponges and cakes, but this walnut cake is one of my favourites. The nuts give it a delicious taste and a lovely moist texture which keeps well.

MAKES 1 × 1 kg (2 lb) CAKE

100 g (4 oz) butter
200 g (7 oz) caster sugar
4 eggs, separated
100 g (4 oz) plain flour
1 teaspoon baking powder

2 tablespoons Grand Marnier
200 g (7 oz) walnuts, lightly crushed

Pre-heat the oven to 190°C/375°F/Gas 5.

Cream the butter and sugar until light and fluffy, then add the egg yolks, followed by the flour, baking powder, Grand Marnier and walnuts. Whisk the egg whites until stiff, then fold them into the mixture. Pour the mixture into a greased and lined 1 kg (2 lb) loaf tin. Bake for about 1 hour until well-risen, golden-brown and cooked through.

Ⓥ

SPANISH BREAD
Jalá Andalucía

Part of our Jewish heritage, Jalá is still made much as it was until the Jews left Spain in the fifteenth century. This recipe was given to me by a cook in Córdoba. She makes this sweet bread to use in bread and butter pudding.

MAKES 2 × 500 g (1 lb 2 oz) LOAVES

4 tablespoons warm water
1 tablespoon caster sugar
50 g (2 oz) yeast
1 kg (2 lb) plain flour
1 teaspoon salt
1 tablespoon olive oil

150 ml (5 fl oz) warm water
2 eggs, beaten
1 egg white
1 tablespoon sesame or
    poppy seeds
2 tablespoons honey

Mix the warm water, sugar and yeast and leave for 10 minutes until frothy. Mix the flour and salt. Add the oil, followed by the yeast mixture, the remaining water and the 2 eggs. Mix together and knead the dough until it is smooth and elastic. Cover with a damp cloth and leave in a warm place until doubled in size.

Pre-heat the oven to 220°C/425°F/Gas 7.

Divide the dough into 8 equal parts and roll into sausage shapes. Plait 3 rolls together. Divide 1 piece into 3, plait it into a smaller plait and lay it on top of the large plait, sealing the ends. Repeat with the other half of the dough. Brush with beaten egg white and sprinkle with sesame or poppy seeds. Place on a greased baking sheet and bake for about 20 minutes until rich golden-brown. Leave to cool, then brush the loaves with honey.

GLOSSARY

Abanda Rice dish cooked in the *paella* pan.

Acedía Dwarf sole. From the same family as the sole but smaller and exclusive to Andalusia, where it is traditionally fried.

Aceite de Oliva Olive oil. Spanish olive oil is almost the only oil or fat used in Spanish cooking and is available in all supermarkets. Virgin olive oil is the juice extracted from the olives by simple pressing and contains the flavour, vitamins and nutrients of the original fruit. Virgin olive oil is graded according to its degree of acidity. The extra has less than 1 per cent acidity and is considered by gourmets to be the finest. The distinct aroma and flavour of virgin olive oil means it is best used as a dressing rather than a cooking oil.

Acelga Swiss chard. Part of the leaf beets family, *acelgas* are a very popular winter vegetable with dark green leaves and white stems, both of which are cooked. If you cannot find chard you can substitute spinach.

Aderezar To season meat, poultry or fish before cooking.

Ajo tierno or **ajete** Garlic shoot. These young garlic shoots can give the most delicate flavour to a dish such as *revuelto de ajos tiernos y cigalas* (scrambled eggs with garlic shoots and Dublin Bay prawns).

Albacora Small tuna common to the Bay of Biscay. The meat is white and less dense than that of the *atún*, or tuna.

Alcachofas The Spanish always use globe artichokes of all sizes, from tiny ones to very large. The former are often sliced and grilled.

Almeja Clam. Try them as you would eat an oyster – with a simple squeeze of lemon, as they do in Spain, or prepared in a parsley and garlic sauce. Of all the varieties available in Spain, the small *coquina* is one of the most favoured.

Alúbias This is the general term applied to dried beans. They can be white (*blancas*) or red (*pintas*).

Anchoas Anchovy. Also known as *boquerón* in Spain, anchovies are eaten fresh, marinated or filleted and canned in olive oil. If you cannot find fresh anchovies, you can substitute whitebait.

Angulas/anguilas Elvers/eels. Baby eels, or elvers, are freshwater fish which reproduce in the deep waters of the Sargasso Sea. Much valued all over Spain, they are at their best cooked in the Basque Country *al pil-pil*, which is a Christmas treat. They are also served in salads, at room temperature or chilled.

Anís An aniseed-flavoured liqueur.

Arroz Rice, or a dish made with rice. Spaniards favour the short-grain *bomba* variety. Long-grain is also grown in southern Spain. For most dishes, short- or medium-grain risotto rice is suitable.

Asador A large charcoal grill. Restaurants in northern Spain that specialize in this form of cooking are called *asadores*.

Atún Tuna. Tuna is grilled, stewed, marinated, or salted and sun-dried to make *mojama* which is served as a starter. The roe is also pressed and salted as an appetizer.

Azafrán Saffron. Made from the dried stigmas of the saffron crocus and, ounce for ounce, more expensive than gold. It confers a supremely subtle flavour and delicate colour to food.

Bacalao Salt cod. To prepare dishes with salt cod, the fish must be soaked first in cold water for between 24 and 36 hours, and the water must be changed at least three times. The art of extracting the salt cannot be learned in a mere day or two – be patient!

Botifarra or **butifarra** A Catalan white or black pork sausage usually seasoned with salt and pepper. *Botifarra* is sold already boiled and can include a variety of different spices.

Brasa, cocinar a la Cooking over the embers of a wood fire. This technique is used extensively in Spanish cooking, especially in the north and in Catalonia. Although it looks easy, cooking *a la brasa* is quite difficult. It is essential to do it over a good, long-burned wood fire. Once the fire has been lit, you have to wait until the wood has burnt to charcoal, which can take quite a long time, and all the flames have died down. Then you put a metal grill over the fire and burn off any bits left on it from the last time you used it, before grilling the meat, vegetables or fish – always separately from each other. If anything catches light, you can either remove it from the grill or raise the grill.

Barbecues are, in effect, just a way of cooking *a la brasa*. For me, both chicken and lamb need to be marinated in oil, a drop of wine vinegar, a herb or two, a clove of garlic, salt and freshly ground black pepper, and should be left in the marinade for 5–6 hours for it to have any effect.

Calamares Squid. Very popular in Spain, squid can be bought in many sizes, from the very small *chipirones*, which are usually prepared in their own ink, to the much larger sizes which are best for cutting into rings and frying, or for stuffing.

Cardo Cardoon. A well-loved Christmas vegetable usually boiled and served with a light béchamel sauce.

Caserío Basque farmhouse.

Cazón Dogfish. A member of the shark family, this fish is very popular in southern Spain, where it is usually marinated before being fried.

Cazuela, cocinar en The *cazuela* is the earthenware casserole and the dish prepared in it. The simple earthenware *cazuelas* are very popular cooking vessels in Spain. They are flameproof, glazed inside and vary in depth from the fairly shallow small ones used for serving *tapas* to deep ones used for preparing dishes such as fish with excellent sauces like *vizcaína*, for example, or meats in sauce. In Castile, they are used for roasting and, on the whole, the oven-baked rice dishes of Catalonia, the Basque Country and the Levante are also prepared in *cazuelas*. Always use a heat diffuser when cooking on top of the stove, as direct contact with the heat can cause the *cazuela* to crack.

Centolla Spider crab. Also called *txangurro* in the Basque Country where, as in Galicia, it is particularly good. The *centolla* differs from the most common British variety in having very small claws, a round body and spindly legs.

Choco Cuttlefish. Often cooked on the grill plate or *plancha* (with garlic and parsley), and served as an appetizer. It is also cooked in stews.

Choricero pepper A variety of green or red pepper. The term is commonly used for dried, sweet red peppers. They can be obtained from Spanish or Italian delicatessens. To reconstitute dried peppers, see *Pimientos*.

Chorizo Pork sausage flavoured with pepper, *pimentón* and garlic. They are available in delicatessens and supermarkets, but a spicy paprika sausage is a similar substitute.

Embutidos Pork butchery. A variety of mainly meat preparations such as *chorizos*, *morcillas* and *botifarras*. The word *embutir* means to stuff or prepare a sausage.

Gamba Prawn. In Spain, these are usually sold cooked or raw in their shell. In Britain you can buy uncooked frozen prawns which simply need to be blanched if they are not going to be cooked during the recipe. *Gambas* are favourites for appetizers. Eat them grilled or *al ajillo*, with olive oil, garlic and a dash of chilli.

Grelo Turnip top. The leaves of the turnip are used almost exclusively in Galician cooking, and when they are young they are called *navizas*. In Britain, you can substitute spinach or spring greens.

Guindilla Small hot chilli peppers which were brought to Spain by the conquistadores.

Jamón Ham. The legs of white or Iberian breeds of pigs are salted and dry cured. *Jamón Serrano* refers to the way Spanish hams were traditionally cured in the mountains. If you cannot find Spanish cured ham, you can substitute Parma or other similar types of ham.

Jerez Sherry. A fortified white wine produced principally from the Palomino grape, grown on dazzling white chalk (*albariza*) soil in the area of Jerez de la Frontera in Cádiz province. It is fractionally blended in the *solera* system, a method by which the wine in barrel that is ready to be bottled is partly bled off and topped up with younger wine from other casks. It must be a minimum of four years old when sold, although many sherries are considerably older.

There are two basic styles: Fino, on which a veil of yeast called the flor grows, preserving the freshness and light colour of the wine; and Oloroso, which is fuller-bodied and darker. Both are naturally dry, and all other types are based on them. Cream sherry is produced by adding sherry made from raisined Pedro Ximenex grapes to Oloroso.

Judías This is the general term for fresh or dried varieties of Columbian beans brought from the New World in the sixteenth century.

Legumbres Apart from the Columbian beans (*judías* or

alúbias), *garbanzos* (chick peas), *habas* (broad beans) and *lentejas* (lentils) have been part of the Spaniards' daily diet since time immemorial.

Morcilla A black sausage flavoured with onions, salt, pepper, cloves and cinnamon. Sometimes rice and pine kernels are also used. *Morcilla* is boiled in water and left to dry. It can be bought in Spanish delicatessens, or you can substitute other similar black puddings.

Olla A deep cooking pot. Also a cooked dish combining many ingredients which can include meat, fish, vegetables and stock.

Paella A large, round, flat, shallow metal vessel with two or more handles used for cooking rice dishes. The base is always broad enough to accommodate the ingredients that complement the rice and which are cooked or part-cooked in it before the rice and liquid are added. The *paella* is shallow so that the rice cooks evenly and does not need to be disturbed during the cooking process.

Pescados y mariscos Fish and shellfish. There is a tremendous variety of fish eaten in Spain, many of which are available in Britain from fishmongers and supermarkets. Among the popular white fish in Spain are sea bass (*lubina*), gilt-head bream (*dorada*) and sea bream (*besugo*), hake (*merluza*), monkfish (*rape*), sole (*lenguado*) and turbot (*rodaballo*). Among the most popular oily fish are anchovy (*anchoa* or *boquerón*), mackerel (*caballa*), red mullet (*salmonete*) and grey mullet (*lisa*), sardines (*sardinas*), swordfish (*pez espada*), trout (*trucha*) and white tuna (*albacora*).

The Spanish love shellfish and other seafood, including

clams (*almejas*), oysters (*ostras*), prawns (*gambas*), and squid (*calamares*). Always use shellfish on the day of purchase.

Picada A Catalan sauce which is used to thicken and enhance the flavour of a dish. It is made by pounding together in a mortar and pestle numerous ingredients such as nuts, bread, garlic and even chocolate.

Pimentón A sweet or hot spice similar to paprika.

Pimientos Capsicum peppers. The red and green varieties were introduced into Spain from South America by the conquistadores and are used extensively in Spanish cooking. *Pimiento morrón* is canned red pepper, available in Britain in many delicatessens. *Piquillo* peppers are small, sweet, pointed red peppers that are sold roasted, in tins. If you cannot find them, use ordinary tinned small red peppers.

Dried red peppers are easily prepared by putting them in cold water, bringing the water to the boil, then draining them and repeating the process. After that you will be able to use a teaspoon to spoon out the flesh from the skin of the peppers.

Puchero A deep, traditionally earthenware, pot which is bulbous in shape, narrowing into a straight neck of varying length. The *puchero* usually has two handles set in the shoulders of the lower part. *Arroz caldoso* is cooked in a *puchero*.

Revuelto Very moist scrambled eggs cooked in a frying-pan, *cazuela* or bain-marie, usually with another ingredient such as garlic shoots, wild mushrooms, prawns or spinach.

Sofrito *Sofrito* is one of Spanish cooking's most important sauces but, contrary to what many people believe, it is not tomato sauce. *Sofrito* is made with 2 to 3 tablespoons of Spanish olive oil; 2 large Spanish onions, peeled and finely chopped; 6 ripe tomatoes, skinned; 1 to 2 tablespoons of water and a pinch of salt.

Heat the oil in a heavy-based metal frying-pan or flameproof earthenware casserole. When it is very hot but not boiling, add the onion. As it cooks it will change texture and colour, turning from transparent to pink then orangey-brown. At this point, not before, add the tomato with or without the seeds, as you prefer. When the tomato is half-cooked, you can add 1 or 2 spoonfuls of water to help it caramelize. When the sauce is ready it will have the consistency of jam, and the secret is to make it in a kitchen ruled by patience and calm!

Txakolí A light, white, slightly pétillant wine which comes from the Basque Country.

Vinagre de Jerez Sherry vinegar. A rich and concentrated vinegar made from sherry in Jerez de la Frontera. Very little sherry vinegar is required to enhance the flavour of a dish.

INDEX

INDEX

INDEX